HOW TO TALK TO FAMOUS PEOPLE

A Memoir
by
Marianne Gage

Azalea Art Press
Sonoma · California

© Marianne Gage, 2024.
All Rights Reserved.

ISBN: 978-1-943471-93-5

Cover Design by Swati Hathi
Author Photo by Paul Fillinger

*Dedicated to my dear Rossmoor Rebels
Jill Reiner, Mary Burkhard, Pat Deisem,
& Robin Moreau*

**Other Books of Interest
by Marianne Gage**

The Wind Came Running
Plainview Press, 2010

The Putneyville Fables
Plainview Press, 2012

All Kinds of Beauty
Azalea Art Press, 2020

The Quirky Kids of Sunshine Hollow
Amazon Publishing, 2022

"That's the whole point of life, you know?
To meet new people."

—*Sherman Alexie*

"Hello there. I'm out social climbing,
but if you leave your name and number,
and if you're anybody, I'll get back to you."

—*Erma Bombeck*

CONTENTS

Introduction   *i*

Chapter 1   1
Charm Bracelets and Cadillacs
Jimmy Jeffries and Greer Garson

Chapter 2   7
Lamb of God and Lady Fair
J. C. Penney
Xavier Cugat

Chapter 3   15
The Gift
Doel Reed
Stan Hoig

Chapter 4   24
Beverly Hills Bogeyman
Vincent Price

Chapter 5   32
Mayonnaise on My Artichoke
Roy Bogas

Chapter 6   38
Land of Heart's Desire
Ed Diffenderfer

Chapter 7 52
Bitter Sweet
Noel Coward
Jeanette MacDonald

Chapter 8 60
Okies at the Opera House
Maria Tallchief
George Balanchine

Chapter 9 69
Honest and Plainspoken
Maurice Logan

Chapter 10 74
Backstage Sage
Melvyn Douglas
Helen Gahagan Douglas

Chapter 11 79
Swimming to Belvedere
Russell Nype
Bishop Pike

Chapter 12 87
Cow Palace Pols
William Scranton

Chapter 13 96
Eagle in One
Dale Robertson
Charles Schulz

Chapter 14 101
The FBI and I
Huey Newton

Chapter 15 110
A Thousand Times
More Magnificent Than Anything
Henry Koerner

Chapter 16 116
Blundering Among the Bierstadts
Paul Mills
Steven Zellerbach

Chapter 17 128
Hindsight
George Shearing
Cynthia Mackay
Ed Mackay

Chapter 18 136
St. Helena Swells
Lord Alexander Hesketh

Chapter 19 142
Thoroughly Modern Mollie
Mollie Poupeney

Chapter 20 149
A Comedy of Errol's
Dakin Matthews

Chapter 21 159
"Age, I Do Abhor Thee"
Mercedes Ruehl

Chapter 22 164
Three Years Sitting on a Rock
Mr. Nakamura

Chapter 23 176
"Hey, Vernon!"
Vernon Alley

Chapter 24 185
Dream Fantasy Finale
All

About the Author 227

Acknowledgments 229

Contact | Book Orders 230

Introduction

Although in later life I was sometimes thrown into the company of famous people, I started life in a tiny town in the Oklahoma panhandle, where fighting dust, and going to church were almost the only pursuits.

It was the thirties, in the middle of the Dust Bowl and during the Great Depression.

Despite the fact that my two older brothers escaped my fate, Mama sent me to the First Methodist church three times a week—Sunday morning, Sunday night, and Wednesday night choir practice.

But I didn't attend only school and Sunday School.

Starting as a young child, I found great happiness in the world of cinema. On windswept Main Street, directly across from the family drugstore, Hoig Drug, was the Gage Theater, where I often went, unaccompanied, from the age of eight. It was where I enjoyed Shirley Temple movies, viewed thousands of Chinese peasants trampled to death in *The Good Earth,* and saw racial issues confronted in *Imitation of Life*. Once, screaming, I was carried out of a Frankenstein movie by my brother Stan, who happened to be there that day.

The contrast between my own life and the lives I saw pictured on the screen was extreme. I wasn't comparing them, simply enjoying the spectacle.

I was a good student, eager to learn, and even won a spelling contest and blue ribbon (proudly displayed by my father on the marble back-bar of the soda fountain) when I was in sixth grade. I was pretty puffed up about it.

Later, during my years at Oklahoma Agricultural & Mechanical College in Stillwater, I became a leader in religious activities, organizing evening vespers in my dorm with candles and a Bible as props. The quintessential good girl, I followed my mother's strictures for twenty-one years, only starting to kick up my heels after college, when I bought a one-way rail ticket for California on the Acheson, Topeka and Santa Fe.

HOW TO TALK TO FAMOUS PEOPLE

Chapter 1

Charm Bracelets and Cadillacs
Jimmy Jeffries & Greer Garson

I've always been a sucker for celebrities.

Politicians, famous writers, business titans, sports figures—and especially movie stars. As a teenager, I was a movie magazine junkie, privy to *Modern Screen, Silver Screen,* and *Screen Romance* via the family drugstore. My parents tried to discourage me, but I ate this stuff up. Hardly anyone else knew that Tyrone Power's wife Annabella cut her own hair with manicure scissors, that Mickey Rooney got married eight times, or that Deanna Durbin sang "Il Bacio" for the studio's vocal coach, then for Louis B. Mayer, who signed her to a contract.

The power of celebrity was demonstrated to me on my ninth birthday when I received a bracelet loaded with miniature silver charms from my Uncle Ed in Texas. Charm bracelets were all the rage in the '40s, and mine jangled with the Eiffel tower, a carved rose, a tiny piano, a radio, and a little plump heart with the name 'Jimmy Jeffries' engraved on it.

When I called Long Distance to thank Uncle Ed, I asked, "Who's Jimmy Jeffries?"

He said, "Don't you listen to *Early Birds*? Jimmy's the biggest radio star we have down here, kiddo! He's a friend of mine, and you oughta be mighty flattered he bought you that charm!"

I had never heard my uncle sound so enthusiastic about anyone, not even the Governor of Texas, Lee O'Daniel, whom he also knew. I found out that more than two million people listened to *Early Birds* every morning.

My father didn't want his breakfast disturbed, but after I got the bracelet, if Daddy wasn't around, Mama and I tuned in to Jimmy's show.

The gift of the bracelet had a bit of fallout when I began showing it off in class. I passed it to Joy Lee, who passed it on to Oletha, who for some reason sneaked it to Bobby Moyers. He snickered loudly and sent it on to Lester Fillcreek.

By then the teacher had noticed the rumble in our section of the classroom. She confiscated the bracelet, and in a decidedly frosty tone, asked whose it was. Crestfallen at being reprimanded, I burst into tears and was sent to the principal's office without the bracelet. Since I couldn't stop bawling, he allowed me to walk home. When I got there I told Mama my sad story, then went outside and climbed my special comfort tree over the dog pen. I stayed there for hours, hungry and martyred, until my brother Stan came home from school and climbed up to where I sat.

"What's wrong?" he asked, folding his long legs around a tree branch.

"Trouble—*not my fault!*" Tears welled up again.

"Whose fault *is* it?"

"Joy Lee and Oletha and Bobby and Lester! And now my bracelet's gone!"

"I've got it here," he said, and he took it out of his pocket and handed it over.

After that, the bracelet somehow lost its charm, and I only wore it on rare occasions. I put it away and only discovered it years later, in time for a woman friend of mine to use it making my favorite necklace of all time. My Mickey Mouse watch and Shirley Temple doll are gone forever,— floating in those hazy mists of the sweepings and filings of childhood.

I was a dreamer as a child, and I don't mean daydreams. My dreams were exciting, dramatic, and sometimes dangerous, and they came when I was asleep in bed.

"You've got way too much imagination," my mother told me one day. "What kind of dream is that for a little girl to have?"

She was ironing a blouse for me to wear to school, and she whipped it off the ironing board and hung it on a hanger. I was finishing my oatmeal, and had just described a dream in which I was floating over our town's rooftops and suddenly landed in a field of briars—with thorns.

"It was like it really happened, Mama! It was really real, and the thorns hurt!"

"Pish-tosh! You had that dream because you ate a whole bowl of strawberries just before you went to bed. I *warned* you that you'd get a stomachache!"

"My stomach didn't hurt one bit. And the dream really *happened*!"

Twenty years later, an even more celebrated star became part of our family lore. By then I had been married for two years to a man who liked to garden and was handy with watering and planting.

Uncle Ed's son, my cousin Sam Keever, had inherited the family undertaking business after my uncle died, and was driving me back to the Dallas airport from Ennis for my return to California. We were traveling in style in his new Cadillac; the funeral home maintained a small fleet of these luxurious cars. I had been visiting Mama, who had migrated to Texas after Daddy died to be near her brothers. She came along for the ride, and as we neared the outskirts of the city, Sam started talking about the members of his hoity-toity Dallas Country Club.

"Why, Greer Garson is a member! She's married to this rich Texas rancher—and *I've met her!* I'm tellin' you, she is one gracious lady. She even writes thank-you notes to her gardener!"

Mama, always ready to puncture anyone's balloon, spoke up from the back seat. "That's nothin'. My daughter *sleeps* with her gardener!"

Sam was silent for the rest of the trip, while I indulged myself with a silent chuckle.

Greer Garson, CBE (Commander of the British Empire), (1904-1996) was a British-American actress who was very popular during the Second World War. She was one of America's top-ten box office draws from 1942-1946.

Born in Manor Park, London, England, of Scottish and Ulster-Scots descent, she was educated at the University of London with the intention of becoming a teacher. Instead she opted to work with an advertising agency. During this time, she appeared in local theatrical productions, gaining a reputation as an extremely talented actress. She was discovered by Louis B. Mayer while he was on a visit to London looking for talent.

Garson was signed to a contract with MGM and appeared in Goodbye, Mr. Chips in 1939. The movie won rave reviews and garnered her a nomination as best actress, the first of six nominations. She was also nominated for Pride and Prejudice and Blossoms in the Dust, and won the Academy Award for Mrs. Miniver, a role she would forever be known by. As Marie Curie in Madame Curie, she would get another nomination, and the same the next year in Mrs. Parkington. She would stay with MGM until 1954.

In 1960 she was cast in the role of Eleanor Roosevelt in Sunrise at Campobello, which landed her seventh Academy Award nomination. Her final appearances on the silver screen were in The Singing Nun and The Happiest Millionaire.

Garson retired to the New Mexico ranch she shared with her husband, millionaire Buddy E.E. Fogelson, concentrating on the environment and other various charities, and died in Dallas, Texas, at 91 years old.

Chapter 2

Lamb of God and Lady Fair
J. C. Penney & Xavier Cugat

By the time I was a senior in college in 1952, I had earned a number of honors, one of which was serving as co-chairman of Religious Emphasis Week.

It wasn't enough that Stillwater had fifty Protestant and Catholic churches; some high-up muckamuck thought we needed to devote a whole week to religion on campus. Renowned individuals, known to be among the faithful, would be coming to speak from all over the U.S. That was fine with me; I was still devotedly and fanatically true to Methodism. I organized nightly devotions in my dorm, and was president of the campus YWCA.

I stayed personally and technically pure as well, only smoking in my dorm room. Still influenced by Mom's teetotalism, not to mention the abstinence pledges I'd signed at Methodist revivals, I imbibed not a single alcoholic drink during college, not even beer.

I agree to abstain from all liquors of an intoxicating quality whether ale, porter, wine, or spirits, except as medicine.

When I learned that I was to introduce Mr. Penney, I went to the library and looked him up. I found that he was born in 1875, so was now in his late seventies. He had come to religion when hearing the hymn "God Will Take Care of You" in a hospital chapel, where he was recovering from a breakdown caused by the stock market crash. After developing a chain of 1400 stores, his personal fortune was gone, and the business was at risk. He borrowed against life insurance policies, which helped the company meet its payroll, and Penney's Stores was saved.

When my brother Stan, a World War II veteran and graduate student on campus, heard that I was going to be co-chairman of Religious Emphasis Week, he called my dorm to give me a hard time.

"Your halo's slippin' a bit, isn't it, for that job?" he snickered. "I saw you yesterday in front of the Life Science building, and you didn't look very religious to me."

I knew I shouldn't ask, but I did.

"What are you talking about?"

"You were wearing those cut-off black pants and that tight sweater!"

Standing at the phone in the chilly corridor, I felt my blood rise. What business was it of his what I wore! I had seen the new Capri pants, introduced by Audrey Hepburn in *Roman Holiday*, in the window of a downtown shop. And what sweater was he talking about? That old green thing I'd worn since junior high?

But Stan wasn't the only one who expressed doubts.

Laughing, my roommate Margie Johnson said, *"You're the co-chairman of Religious Emphasis Week? You were just confessing to me about your animal behavior with Marty Wallhanger! I don't think you're pure enough to occupy the stage with that God-fearing old man."*

Why had I ever told her about how Harvey and I had necked for a solid hour, steaming up all his car windows.

That settled it. No more confessions, to Margie or anyone else.

Mr. Penney and I met for the first time backstage. He was a stately, reserved gentleman, so subdued and restrained that I considered loosening him up with a joke I'd heard recently.

"Why does your girlfriend wear a fur-bottomed nightgown?"

"To keep her neck warm."

I had told the joke to my parents the last time I went home, and at this portent of my incipient corruption, Daddy looked embarrassed, Mama left the room, and they later discussed pulling me out of college.

Luckily I decided not to tell the joke. Instead I smiled, shook Mr. Penney's hand, and asked if he'd had a pleasant trip.

In front of the auditorium full of students, I stood and made my introduction. It went smoothly except for one thing; I had practiced so hard at getting his initials right that I got them wrong.

"And now I would like to introduce Mr. P. J. Penney!"

His talk was about religion as a force in his life, but I have no recollection of his words.

I read later that he'd once met with a young Sam Walton, training him to wrap packages with the minimum amount of paper and ribbon. Now *that* was a meaningful encounter.

For contrast with Penney, a month later I met Hollywood celebrities Xavier Cugat and Abbe Lane.

I was shocked when my dorm chose me and two other girls, one from each floor of Willard Hall, to compete in the Aggie yearbook beauty contest. The pageant was always judged by a visiting celebrity, and it was a big deal, almost as earthshaking as the yearly basketball championship. Basketball legend, seven-foot Bob Kurland, wasn't at A&M now, but I knew his sister Delores, who was a mere six feet. If chosen, my picture would go in the REDSKIN yearbook, and I knew brother Stan would be impressed.

Not if I won, because of course I wouldn't, but that I was even in the running.

I was impressed that I was in the running!

Girls represented each sorority and dorm, and six or so represented the townie girls. We arrived at the student union, 35 or 40 of us, to be judged by Cugat and Abbe, his gorgeous blonde band singer. They stood together at a small podium, both of them smiling and friendly.

I didn't know it at the time, but Abbe was younger than me by a year.

Before the judging, a bunch of us crowded into the girls' restroom, trying to make sure our stocking seams were straight and our makeup and hair up to snuff. I didn't know anything about hairdressers at that stage in my life, and didn't use any makeup other than lipstick. Hardly anyone else did either. I noticed one girl, Trudy Gallagher from another dorm, was wearing a lot of mascara, but she was the exception.

A girl I'd never seen before was wearing what was obviously a blond wig, and another, no doubt one of the rich sorority girls from Tulsa or Oklahoma City, was wearing a fur coat over a two-piece bathing suit. I couldn't decide if these two would be victorious because of their extra glamour, or would look like affected frauds.

I was watching Marsha Culpepper stuffing falsies down her bra when the door opened and Abbe Lane walked in. We all stopped our primping and stood transfixed as this ultimate glamour girl smiled, opened the door of one cubicle and stepped in. It was shocking to share space with one of our judges, but I became embarrassed by our silence.

I decided I should say something to lighten the moment, so I walked to the space where Abbe had disappeared and said in a loud stage whisper, "These toilets back up, so be careful!"

Everyone tittered, and I realized I had possibly said the wrong thing. Beet red, I left, and most of the girls followed. As I recall, no one looked in my direction for the duration of the event.

Xavier Cugat was a plump man with a sweep of black hair, a slick lock falling over one eye. He had a small moustache and an oozing smile, and since I'd always been a slave to movie magazines, I knew a lot about him.

He was born in Spain and raised in Cuba; his orchestra had played at the Waldorf Astoria in New York all through World War II; and he had a restaurant on Hollywood's "Restaurant Row." He was quoted as saying that George Burns and Milton Berle loved *chile verde*. I'd seen him and his orchestra in several movies with Esther Williams, and his recordings of "Perfidia" and "Brazil" were two of the biggest hits of the 1940's.

The name 'Cugat' oozed with celebrity, and here I was, in the same room with him! I was the last to march by, I don't remember why. Maybe we drew for places, and I came up with the last number. I wore a red dress, which I thought would get some attention, and as I stumbled past, I murmured the cliché *'Last but not least'* accompanied by a deranged smile.

I've had to live with the memory of that and the toilet remark all these years.

I came in twelfth, and a small picture of me was printed in the yearbook, along with big pictures of the top ten. Paula Sue Neiswonger—Kappa, Theta, Chi Omega, I'm not sure which—was the most beautiful by far.

My brother was impressed with my achievement, but his only comment was, "Nice goin', kid."

I didn't go to the dance Cugat's band put on that night, and I never saw him in another movie—maybe his star was already beginning to fade. He and Abbe divorced, and later he married Charo, who was more bombastic and bosomy than Abbe. After she became famous, Charo was quoted as saying, "Around the world I am known as a great musician. But in America I am known as the 'cuchi-cuchi' girl. That's okay, because cuchi-cuchi has taken me all the way to the bank!"

Her mentor and husband Cugat was quoted as saying, "I would rather play Chiquita Banana and have my swimming pool than play Bach and starve."

> *James Cash Penney* (1875–1971) *began working for a small chain of stores in the western United States called the Golden Rule Stores in 1898. In 1902, the owners offered him one-third partnership in a new store. Penney invested $2,000, and by 1929, the number of his stores reached 1400. He died in 1971, and Dr. Norman Vincent Peale delivered the eulogy. Penny's estate was valued at approximately $35 million.*

Xavier Cugat *(1900-1990) was a Spanish-American bandleader and native of Spain who spent his formative years in Havana, Cuba. His family immigrated to Cuba when Xavier was five. He was trained as a classical violinist and played with the Orchestra of the Teatro Nacional in Havana. Cugat appeared in recitals with Enrico Caruso, playing violin solos. A trained violinist and arranger, he was a leading figure in the spread of Latin music in U.S. popular music.*

In New York, he was the leader of the resident orchestra at the Waldorf-Astoria before and after World War II. He was also a cartoonist and restaurateur. Cugat recorded on Columbia Records, RCA Victor, Mercury, and Decca. Dinah Shore made her first recordings as vocalist with Cugat in 1939, and in 1940, his recording of "Perfidia" became a big hit. He made records for the conga, the mambo, the cha-cha-cha, and the twist. "Brazil" was also a big hit, reaching No. 17 in the Billboard Top 100.

Chapter 3

The Gift
Doel Reed

I couldn't have been greener when I first arrived in Stillwater in the fall of 1948. Growing up in the panhandle, I had done a lot of drawing and had dabbled in watercolor, but never, in our hamlet of 750 souls, had I taken an art lesson or attended an art class. There weren't any. Nevertheless, based on my talent for drawing, I started college with plans to become a great artist.

Besides classes in the basic requirements for a Bachelor of Arts degree, I signed up for drawing and painting, and continued with three-hour labs in those subjects for all four years. In the last two years I began to learn lithography, aquatint, and etching, classes taught by Doel Reed, the head of the Art Department.

He was a tall, bald, imposing man with a touch of arrogance, and we students never questioned his authority.

We were especially impressed that he was part of an artist's colony in Taos, New Mexico. He told us he went there every summer to paint and print.

I had the feeling that Mr. Reed believed in me, that he thought I had a gift that needed developing. In my junior year he gave me a special assignment for advanced credit, asking me to make drawings of representatives of the Indian tribes on campus. I don't know how he acquired the models, but I assumed it was because he had connections to other college departments. My models were all young men; later I wondered if the Indian girls weren't allowed or didn't want to pose.

As I recall, these were the tribal boys I drew: Shawnee, Caddo, Cherokee, Chickasaw, Choctaw, Potawatamie, Comanche, Kickapoo, and Kiowa.

I finished the Conté crayon drawings, but as far as I know, nothing was ever done with them. Maybe they weren't good enough.

When I was a senior, one of my lithographs of an old wagon was used in the college literary magazine, and Mr. Reed told me it was his doing. I was thrilled; nothing of mine had ever been published before, so I sent copies to my parents and a few other relatives.

I began to notice that Reed's special treatment was accompanied by personal interest. Once, when somewhere he saw a picture of me with my date for a dance—another art student, skinny and mustached—he took me aside and said, "You can do better than that."

I was shocked that he would make such a personal remark, and I responded, *"I don't want to do better."*

In other words, stay out of my business.

He raised his chin, gave me that gimlet-eyed, haughty look that was his specialty, and walked away.

Suddenly it was June, and I was graduating. I was incredulous when told that, since I was vice-president of the senior class, I would be leading the group on their march into the auditorium. Manny Blenheim, our president and an architecture student, hadn't fulfilled all the requirements for graduation, so I was next in line to do the job.

On the final day of class, Professor Reed said, "Come by my studio before you leave town. I have something for you."

"Where's your studio?".

"Do you know where City Hall is, downtown? I'm two doors away."

"Okay," I said. He told me the address, and I wrote it down.

Graduation day arrived, and I was upset and disappointed because my dad wasn't coming for my big day. Uncle Nard and Aunt Addie were coming all the way from Texas to attend with Mom, but not Daddy. When Mom called the night before to tell me, I whined, "Can't he close the drugstore for just one day?"

Mom said it was his heart, and that he'd had an incident or two lately.

The big day was only minimally affected by a marching protest group. Student protests weren't common then anywhere in the U.S., and especially not on an Oklahoma campus. However, a group of architecture students wanted to show their displeasure at their pal's exclusion from the job I'd been named to. Zizi Fellhazen was the only one of the malcontents I knew; she lived in Willard Hall on my floor. Zizi, a petite and ultra-smart redhead, was a character from New Orleans who had previously been reprimanded by the dean for helping paint the founder's statue red just before Founder's Day. I knew her as one of the few girls who got away with drinking beer in her room. Considering the iron hand of our housemother, Mrs. Pope, that was truly an achievement.

Zizi and the other four, all guys, turned up wearing chains of onions and FREE MANNY signs around their necks. It was ridiculous, but I suppose it made them feel better. The stench was the worst part of it, lending a bad odor to the ceremony.

I ignored them, only wanting to get on with things and get out of there, and I think everyone else felt the same. Without another hitch or glitch, the speeches and awarding of diplomas went on for a full two hours.

When it was over, I shed my cap and gown and started looked for family. I couldn't find them, but Stan met me and said, "I'm driving you back to Fairfax."

"Where's Mom?"

"They already left."

"Okay, but first I have to pick up my stuff at the dorm, then go by Professor Reed's studio. He wants to see me about something."

"You mean that old bald guy? What's he want to see you about?"

"Dunno, but I have the address," I said, flourishing the slip of paper.

I knew that if I hadn't sound assertive, he would have overruled my wishes.

Stan helped me carry several loads of clothes, books, paintings, and other detritus to his old Chevy, then we drove to downtown Stillwater and found the address. We parked, and with Stan waiting in the car, I knocked on the studio door.

"Come in!"

Professor Reed was wearing the blue smock he always wore for teaching.

"I was just cleaning up." He laughed, but I detected a nervous wobble in the sound.

I looked around. His studio was filled with two painting easels, a printing press, and tables piled with items related to a working artist's life. Overflowing bookshelves lined the room, and art quartos were stacked high on chairs.

"I can only stay a few minutes," I said. "My brother's waiting outside; he's driving me home."

He gazed at me in surprise, his expression showing disappointment. He threw back his head, eyes hooded, then reached out a hand and touched my shoulder.

"I had hoped, after all these years of knowing one another, that you might give me some of your time."

What was this?

I made an effort to keep my mouth from dropping open. This icon, this institution, was begging me to spend time with him. But he had a wife and daughter, and he was old!

I walked a few steps away, shrugging off his hand.

"Sorry, I can't. I know I owe you a lot, sir—Mr. Reed—but my brother wants me to—"

"I understand."

He stood rooted to the spot for another few seconds, then walked to a cabinet of wide drawers against the wall.

"I wanted to give you this, from my work in Taos."

He opened the top drawer and pulled out an aquatint of a Taos church. I had seen this subject matter before in art publications he left lying around the art lab.

"Oh!"

"I'll wrap it for you. Try to have it framed soon, will you? Don't let it lie around."

"Of course not! I'll treasure it forever!"

He taped the print to heavy cardboard with some sort of special tape, then put it in a large art sleeve and handed it to me.

Once again he put his hand on my shoulder. "You don't have any idea—"

Why did his voice sound so tremulous, like leaves shaking in the wind?

I backed away. How long had he felt this way about me? And did he always form an attachment to one of his female students? If so, I had no doubt he would soon find someone else.

I decided to be kinder, and besides, what I was about to say was true.

"I can't thank you enough, Professor! All the things I learned from you in my time here, I'll never forget them! And I'll never, ever forget you!" I was sidling toward the exit as I spoke. "So—goodbye!"

"Goodbye. Here, let me get the door."

Clasping the blotter under one arm, I reached out with my other hand, and we shook hands in farewell.

Outside, Stan opened the trunk, and I slid the print on top of my suitcase, then got in the car.

"What did the old fool want?" he asked, turning the key in the ignition.

I couldn't answer at first, but finally mumbled, "Gave me one of his prints."

As we drove out of town I began to sob, and I didn't stop until many miles later.

I recently checked with a Taos gallery, and my aquatint is worth thousands. But I would never part with it.

Doel Reed *(1894-1985)* was born in Indiana and raised in Indianapolis. He took his first art lessons at the John Herron Art Museum while in grade school. In 1916 he studied at the Art Academy in Cincinnati, Ohio with L.H. Meaken, James Hopkins and H.H. Wessel. Reed served with the 47th Infantry, 4th Division during World War 1 and was stationed in France between 1919 and 1920. Reed married Elizabeth Jane Sparks, a watercolor artist, and they had a daughter, Martha, who later became a well-known dress designer in Taos. He was made a full member of the National Academy of Design in 1952 as a graphic artist. He taught printmaking at Oklahoma State University between 1924 and 1959 in Stillwater, Oklahoma before moving to join the artists' community in Taos, New Mexico in 1959, where he had previously spent summers. He was a member of the National Academy of Design; the Allied Artists of America; Audubon Artists; the Chicago Society of Etchers; the Indiana Print Makers; Prairie Print Makers; the California Printmakers Society, to name a few. He exhibited extensively throughout the U.S. and collaborated on the publication *Doel Reed Makes an Aquatint*, 1965. He died in Taos, New Mexico.

Stan Hoig *(1924-2008)* was employed by the University of Central Oklahoma in 1964 (then Central State College) as a journalism professor. He regaled his students with stories of Oklahoma and inspired them to be writers and thus became one of the *campus's most popular lecturers. Born in Duncan, Oklahoma, and raised in Gage, Professor Hoig loved the state's history and wrote about it until his death in 2009. He published 23 books on Oklahoma's western heritage and particularly about its Native American ancestry; he contributed to a host of encyclopedias on western, Native American, and Oklahoma history and produced four local histories, primarily about Edmond and Central State.*

Through his extensive publications, Stanley Hoig earned numerous writing awards: Clement E. Trout Writing Award (OSU), U.S. Treasury Department Award, two Muriel H. Wright Awards (from Oklahoma Historical Society), Distinguished Scholar Award (American Association of University Professors), the Ralph Ellison Lifetime Achievement Award from the Oklahoma Center for the Book, and The Myers Center Award for his Trail of Tears book (given for "outstanding work on intolerance"). Other Hall of Fame awards received by Dr. Hoig include: Edmond (1990), Oklahoma Journalism (1994) and Oklahoma Historians (1997).

Chapter 4

Beverly Hills Bogeyman
Vincent Price

It was time for me to leave. I'd finished college, and California was beckoning.

I had a girl cousin in the Bay Area and a brother in Los Angeles. Maybe they could put up with me until I got my bearings. My plan was to get a job, then do more graduate work in art on my pathway to fame.

Maybe I could even meet a nice guy, someone more sophisticated then the fellow Methodists, farmers, and engineers I'd dated in college, none of whom came up to my standards.

What were my standards, anyway? Never mind, I'd know when I met him.

Mama and Daddy didn't want me to go. Daddy made noises about promising to stay out of my love life if I stayed, and Mama said, "I'd worry about you bein' out there with all those earthquakes!"

I said, "What about all the tornados *here?*"

We'd had one that blew through south of town in 1947, the famous Woodward tornado.

I had hardly any money and planned, come Hell or High-Water, to take the bus, but finally with financial help from Mama and Stan, who contributed $50, I boarded the Atchison, Topeka & Santa Fe *California Limited* in Oklahoma City, then headed west.

As I recall, it was a very long train ride, two days and a night.

I couldn't afford a berth, and happened to sit next to a lovely old man from Tennessee. During the long ride we chatted, going back and forth together to the dining car, or reading or sleeping in our chairs, and the endless rackety-rack of the train's wheels was extraordinarily conducive to sleep. The old man's daughter lived in Long Beach, and was going through a divorce. He said he wanted to be with her, to help her get through it.

I had thought all porters were black men, but we had a white porter on board, Oliver, who was very friendly. I was thrilled to be starting a new chapter in life, and brimful with the joy of living, so I was friendly back.

Porters handled luggage and attended to lots more duties on board, but it seemed as if Oliver had a lot of time on his hands. I would look around, and there was middle-aged Oliver.

"Need anything, Miss? Would you like me to reserve a dining seat for you? Need any hand lotion? *Peanuts?*"

When we finally arrived at Union Station in L.A., the old man and I hugged as we said goodbye, while Oliver watched from the train steps.

"Why are you saying goodbye to your father?" he asked.

"Arthur's not my father. Did you think he was my father?"

His look of consternation was almost funny.

What would Oliver have done if he'd known the man wasn't my relation?

"Oh, there's my brother!" I yelled.

I turned and threw Oliver a kiss goodbye.

I loved my brother Mel, and was anxious to spend time with him and his family. He and June had two little girls. My brothers were an integral part of my growing-up years, of course. Stan, six years older, often made me the butt of his own unhappiness, but I learned to cope with that. When I was around twelve, Stan and I were playing checkers in the rear of the drugstore. When I unexpectedly won a game, he threw the checkerboard and all the checkers in my face and stomped away.

That night I had one of my dreams.

Stan was driving Daddy's old Model T Ford, and I was in the passenger seat. We were delivering a prescription to old Mr. Grigg's' farm, and Stan was yelling at me about something, and all at once I yelled back, "*Shut up!*"

Instead of punching me in the arm, he speeded up, and we swerved off the road and into a barbed-wire fence.

I wasn't hurt one bit, but Stan had a broken nose.

Mel, ten when I was born, always had time to swing me in the backyard swing, or if I skinned a knee, he put on a bandage.

When I was a teenager he taught me how to drive, and during WWII, sent me money from North Africa and Italy, where he was a crew chief on P-38s. He met June at a USO canteen in Los Angeles before he went overseas, and after the war moved to California, got married, and on the GI Bill, went to USC to become an engineer. Now he had a job with the city of Los Angeles. He said he spent most of his working days buying up land for the growing freeway system.

There was an earthquake that first night in Encino. When the house shook as if made of matchsticks in the middle of the night, Melvin said to June in bed, "Just wait a minute, Marianne's going to appear at that door."

And I did.

"That wasn't just one of your crazy dreams, Sis," Mel said. "That was a real California earthquake!"

Even though I eventually settled in Northern California, my first weeks out of college were spent in Los Angeles, trying to find a teaching job. But every time I was turned loose in L.A., I ended up feeling lost, friendless, and abandoned. Having always lived in small towns, the transportation system of the huge metropolis totally bewildered me. Mel was too busy to drive me to job interviews. My sister-in-law was needed at home with their two little girls, De De and Judy, and I didn't know another soul in the huge sprawling city.

Somehow, one hot August day I ended up in a posh Wilshire Boulevard art gallery in Beverly Hills. I don't know what had impelled me to go there, but it was more enjoyable than enduring a long bus ride to the Los Angeles Public School Offices way out to Hell-and-Gone.

I have a dim recollection of Matisse paintings, my first glimpse of authentic French Art. But I had been drawing and painting for four years and had studied Art History for a couple of semesters. What else was there for me to know?

As I wandered around the gallery wearing my blue-checked gingham dress, reminiscent of Dorothy in *The Wizard of Oz*, I became aware that the actor Vincent Price was pacing about also. I had read that Price was an art expert, and I felt exalted just being in his company. Having perused movie magazines for years, not only did I know the names of every prominent actor in Hollywood, I knew their spouses, hobbies, and most famous roles. I had seen Mr. Price in *The Song of Bernadette, Laura,* and *Leave Her to Heaven*, but somehow missed *Abbott and Costello Meet Frankenstein*.

Price never looked in my direction, but I kept stealing furtive glances at him.

My life so far had been a combination of stepping forward and stepping back. There were times when I hesitated to take a leadership position for fear that I wasn't up to the challenge and, faced with certain situations, I would became frozen into inaction. Contrarily, on some occasions I would exhibit an unbelievable amount of *chutzpah* (a word my dorm pal Rachel Vashinsky had taught me).

I stepped toward him and said, "Mr. Price, forgive me, but I was reading about your new movie in the *Valley Times* this morning. Are you enjoying making *House of Wax?*"

He was standing in front of a Matisse study of a woman in a green hat.

Slowly, he turned his head in my direction. "I beg your pardon?"

I looked around at the empty gallery, wondering who else he thought I might be talking to.

"Yes. I read about you just yesterday, and I was wondering, do you like working in 3-D?"

Finally he spoke. "I came here, Miss, to look at the art, and I don't care to comment about my film work. What I *do* prefer is to be left alone."

"Oh, sure! *Sorry.* I was just wondering, it's such a new medium and all. That's what the paper said."

He glared at me anew, and feeling totally chastened, I stumbled to the other side of the room. Price left the gallery a few minutes later, and I glimpsed him pouring his long lean body into the back of a limousine.

Disappointed that my attempt at friendship had been thwarted, on the bus ride back to Encino I made up a mock conversation between us.

> *ME:*
> *I'm from out of town, Mr. Price, but I've been a lifelong fan. What do you think of Henri Matisse? Personally, I think he's over-rated, and so did Doel Reed, my art professor in Oklahoma.*
>
> *PRICE:*
> *What do you know about it? And I'd rather not talk, if you don't mind.*
>
> *ME:*
> *I'm auditioning for a newspaper job at the L.A. Times, so please think of this as a mini-interview. How do you justify your praise for a man who used every color on his palette and who really didn't draw very well?*
>
> *PRICE:*
> *You're one brash little bitch, aren't you—besides being hopelessly ignorant. Where do you get off approaching me?"*
>
> *ME:*
> *We're the only people here. And I'm a former art student at Oklahoma Agricultural & Mechanical College, so I think I have the right to ask you what the basis for your opinions are.*

PRICE:
I'm leaving, and I'll never darken the door of this gallery again! Goodbye!

That evening I didn't mention my encounter with Vincent Price to Mel. He always thought I didn't know my place in the world, and this would only serve to prove him right.

Vincent Price *(1911–1993) was an American actor known for his distinctive voice and performances in horror films. He has two stars on the Hollywood Walk of fame, one for motion pictures and one for television. Price was an art collector and consultant with a degree in art history; he lectured and wrote books on the subject, and was a noted gourmet cook. His first venture into the horror genre was in the 1939 Boris Karloff film Tower of London. He established himself in the film Laura opposite Gene Tierney, later reuniting with Tierney in Dragonwyk and Leave Her to Heaven. Price studied Art History at Yale University, and was a noted art lover and collector. He worked as an art consultant for Sears-Roebuck, and from 1962 to 1971, Sears offered the "Vincent Price Collection of Fine Art", selling 50,000 fine art prints to the public. Vincent and Mary Grant Price donated 90 pieces from their own art collection and a large sum of money to establish the Vincent Price Art Museum, East Los Angeles College, Monterey Park, California. The collection contains over 9,000 pieces, and is valued at $5 million.*

Chapter 5

Mayonnaise on My Artichoke
Roy Bogas

When I moved into my tiny room on Benvenue Avenue in Berkeley, I was ecstatic. (Twenty-two years later, in 1974, Patti Hearst would be kidnapped from a house not far from there.)

At last I was on my own, with a job at an insurance company as a typist and file clerk, and in my personal life, no one looking over my shoulder telling me what to do. This was a brand-new feeling. I had a married cousin in Oakland, Fran, who watched over me, but she never told me how to behave, even though I lived in her basement, ate her food, and wore her clothes for many weeks.

I was used to being the object of Fran's charity. While I was growing up in the Dust Bowl, Aunt Franka, my dad's sister, had occasionally sent me beautiful clothes Fran had outgrown. My parents had very little money, and Aunt Franka was married to a J.C. Penney executive.

We shared a family resemblance, but my hair was almost black while hers was reddish-brown, and she was slimmer than I. She had beautiful grey-green eyes which looked upon the world with disenchantment, dashed hopes, and a sizeable dose of cynicism.

Fran even took time to drive me to job interviews, and one day, after hiring someone to watch her four young children, drove me up a long winding road behind the UC campus for an interview at the Berkeley Radiation Lab. I wasn't up to their standards, but Allstate would welcome my meager skills a few days later.

After I rented my room, which cost $20 a month, the next question was where would I eat? I shared a bathroom down the hall, but my place had no kitchen, not even a hotplate. The landlord recommended a boarding house, the Chateau de Longpré around the corner on Hillegass, so I signed up for one meal a day.

The boarding house was infinitely more attractive than the house I lived in, although we had a turret. A large, brown-shingled home, the self-styled chateau had broad wooden steps in front, a spacious porch, and a homey ambience within. The street was attractive, with more brown-shingled houses and abundant trees and shrubbery.

There were a number of young men and woman my age who ate there, mostly grad students or working stiffs, and I soon made a few friends. I especially warmed to Harriet, a public health nurse from Canada, and a girl named Edwina who was working on her doctorate in archeology.

A young classical pianist ate there too, no doubt paying for board with his music. His name was Roy Bogas, and he never spoke a word. He was skinny and dark, shy and stand-offish. Maybe he just didn't want to bother with the rest of us. Occasionally he performed on the grand piano in the living room, playing mostly Chopin. Chopin was one of the few composers I knew about, and I was an eager listener. We sat or stood in clusters, enjoying his artistry. My favorite listening place was a small sofa in a corner of the room. Its cushions were soft and welcoming, and I felt secure there.

In those days, what is now called low self-esteem we called an inferiority complex, and I think I must have suffered from some of the symptoms. I had possessed a great deal of confidence back home, due to growing up in a small town where everyone knew me. In college, too, I was blessed with a healthy amount of self-assurance. But now I was convinced that everyone was far above me in culture, money, background, and imminent possibilities. I especially felt humbled when it came to education; everyone seemed to be either working on a master's or a PhD.

Never mind, I thought, once I get my California teaching credential, there will be no more hanging my head. I planned to go back to school as soon as I earned some money. In the meantime, I kept up a facade of boldness, even braggadocio.

I seldom mentioned where I was from, and even though I was trying to get rid of my Okie twang, I probably hadn't. There wasn't anyone else from the South or Southwest—everyone was from some sophisticated metropolis like Walla Walla or Minneapolis. Sheila, a girl from London studying for a master's in political science, spoke in the most aristocratic tones I'd ever heard outside of the movies. I would have liked to be her friend, but she seemed much too suave and golden to ever want to hang out with me.

We sat at tables for four, with white tablecloths and cloth napkins. The menu was stock American fare, nothing elegant. No Crown Roast of Lamb, no Cherries Jubilee. Our waiters passed meat, potatoes, and vegetables, often a nourishing tomato soup or corn chowder, sometimes a tossed salad. Now and then we had spaghetti and meat balls.

One fall evening I was sitting with Harriet, Edwina, and Roy Bogas. Harriet wore her usual twin sweater set, her brown hair held back by barrettes, and Edwina was dressed even more conservatively, in a lace-trimmed blouse with knitted vest and pleated skirt. Through horn-rimmed spectacles, she gazed at the world like a frightened deer. For some reason I had decided to wear my new red party dress, and was unquestionably the most glaring object in the room.

I saw Sheila a few tables away, smiling and laughing with her tablemates. Roy and Edwina were silent as Harriet and I chatted about Richard Nixon's Checkers speech, broadcast on television the night before.

Just then the waiter placed in front of us plates bearing objects I'd never seen before; strange, large-leafed things which looked utterly daunting. Presuming that this was salad, and since there was a big bowl of mayonnaise in the center of the table, I began spooning dollops of it on top of my leafy lump while whispering to Harriet, "What *is* this?"

"An artichoke."

Roy asked, "What are you doing?"

"Eating my artichoke," I said, in a tone that suggested 'Isn't it obvious?'

I continued spreading mayo over the strangely-shaped leaves.

He said, "I've never seen anyone eat an artichoke that way."

My face turned the color of my dress, but I stuck to my guns. "I *always* eat mine like this." For emphasis, I peeled off one of the blades and stuck it in my mouth.

When the three of them finally stopped looking in my direction, I removed it, realizing that if I swallowed any part of the spiky thing, I could choke to death. After that I copied my tablemates, and a few minutes later the waiter removed our leaf-piled plates.

Thankfully, I knew how to eat everything else that was put in front of me. The main course was stewed chicken, and dessert was berry pie with ice cream. We'd had tons of that stuff back home.

For weeks, I seethed at Roy's rude questioning of my table manners. I tried to think of a way to get even, so I stopped going to his piano concerts.

I don't know if he noticed.

> **Roy Bogas** *(1942—   ) is a pianist of international renown, debuting with the San Francisco Symphony at age 14. He became accompanist for violinist Yehudi Menuhin at age 19, playing over a hundred concerts with him throughout North and South America. Roy received piano training in New York and at the San Francisco Conservatory of Music. He was a prizewinner at the Tchaikovsky Competition in Moscow, making his New York and London debuts the following year.*
>
> *In addition to recital work, he has performed as soloist with virtually every orchestra in California, as well as many other orchestras in this country and abroad. Roy studied conducting in Vienna. Fellow classmates included Zubin Mehta and Claudio Abbado. He became Music Director at Holy Names University and remained there for many years. Roy is the founder and director of the MasterGuild Series of professional chamber music, as well as the Gualala Summer Festival of Chamber Music. You can download his performances on I-Tunes.*

Chapter 6

Land of Heart's Desire
Ed Diffenderfer

As I walked around the campus, which was dotted with buildings old and new, I felt as if I had arrived in the land of my dreams. I had no idea that I would soon be meeting the man of my dreams as well.

Or, rather, two of them.

I needed only a few more college units for my teaching credential, so I enrolled at Oakland's California College of Arts & Crafts at College and Broadway, to acquire them. The school was a short bus ride from my Berkeley room, and I could take the classes at night. I intended to keep my job at the insurance office, since I had to pay tuition and I also had to eat.

I enrolled in a painting class, a jewelry class, and a graduate course in art history.

It only strikes me now how utterly lacking in women the faculty was at CCAC in the fifties. There had been only one woman on the art faculty at Stillwater, but in those days no one thought about it, wrote about it or, supposedly, even cared. Ella Jack was the tough old broad who taught watercolor, and I studied under her for two semesters. She didn't give an inch, and now I know why she was so hard-boiled. In that milieu of male domination, she had to seem invulnerable.

CCAC in the fifties wasn't much different. I could be wrong, but I don't remember a single woman among the roster of instructors.

By the time I became a literature student at Cal State Hayward in the late '70s and early '80s, things had improved, and there were several women professors in the English Department.

This could be the time to relate something that happened to me in my senior year at A&M. I needed more units in science in order to graduate, and since I hated science, I put off earning them until my final year. I noticed that Geography could count as a science, and since I'd always wanted to learn more about the world, I decided to take the course being offered.

When I showed up the first day, the instructor asked to speak to me when class was over. As we stood outside the door, his words came out haltingly.

"Uh, Miss, I'm sorry, but this class is really just for men."

"What do you mean? I need the units! And it's listed in the catalogue like any other course."

"I know, but you see—" He cleared his throat and said, "You see, we cover some things that could be embarrassing for a woman."

"Embarrassing for a *woman!* It's a geography class!"

I flounced away before he could reply.

I showed up for the next session and the next, the only girl. I stayed for the entire semester, and the only time I felt embarrassed was when the instructor talked about all the cow dung the Chinese people used to build up their agriculture economy, hauling it from the cities to and fro and here and there, wherever it would do the most good.

We spent three days on Chinese cow shit.

At CCAC my painting professor Mr. Boratko was a Van Dyke-bearded, middle-aged fellow whose teaching techniques weren't much different from those at Stillwater. The most interesting thing about his class was Mark, a handsome young man who set my pot a-boiling. He was tall and dark-haired, worked for his father at a box company, and was a part-time student. To me, he exuded cool sophistication.

That was what I was looking for!

One evening a few weeks after the class started, Professor Boratko offered me a ride home, since he lived in Berkeley too. I said no, I was meeting someone for coffee.

"Mark?" he asked.

Blushing, I nodded.

"What a good-looking fellow! Reminds me a lot of John Gilbert, the silent movie star. Ever heard of him?"

"Yes, I saw him in *The Big Parade*," I replied.

"Didn't know you went back that far."

"We had a movie theater in my hometown, about the only thing we had to do for entertainment, and once in a while they would run a silent film. That's how I know about John Gilbert."

Later that night in Mark's car, when I passed on the compliment, he said he'd never heard of the actor, and we immediately resumed our make-out session. We'd been dating for several weeks, and I was having a hard time holding on to my eternal virgin status. I was pretty sure Mark wouldn't put up with my resistance much longer.

Once he said, "You're really uptight!" Another time he sighed, "Only so far, huh, kiddo?" and took me home without speaking another word.

My jewelry class was taught by bushy-bearded Bob Winston, who became well-known later both as a sculptor and jewelry designer, noted for his revival of the lost-wax casting technique used in ancient Egypt. He made metal jewelry with organic forms and textures. I only knew him as a nice guy who dressed like an early hippie, someone who could help me get closer to my credential.

After six weeks of learning basic jewelry-making techniques, we were given a choice of what to create, and I decided to make a set of cufflinks for Mark. They were my first, last, and only creation, and I thought they were beautiful—oval cat's eye stones set in silver. The materials cost me two days' salary, but I didn't care.

Art history was taught by Professor Helmet Hungerland. I thought he was German because he sounded like all the Nazi movies I'd ever seen. We covered mostly mid-century European art, delving into an overview of contemporary art toward the end of the semester. Our grades would hinge on a typed paper written about an artist of our own choosing. After thinking it over, I chose Georges Rouault, a French artist I'd always admired for his religious subject matter. Weekends I made trips to the downtown Berkeley library, researching and writing. Too gutless to use the typewriter at work, I borrowed one from my boarding-house pal Harriet, and in the end I was proud of my 1500-word treatise.

The day came for reading our papers, and I was excited and nervous. Ten of us sat in a circle, with the professor sitting among us. Two others preceded me. Bill Strickland read his paper about Jacques Louis David. Bill's reading voice was high and squeaky; I could tell he was more nervous than I was.

Then Carol Weeks read, in her shrill New York accent, her take on Caspar David Friedrich, a German painter.

My reading went beautifully, and I was sure that the other students were impressed. After all, I had an academic for a brother, and no doubt some of it had rubbed off.

There was one hitch. I wasn't absolutely certain of how to pronounce my subject's name, so I did it phonetically, 'ROO-ALT'.

I covered Rouault's years as a glass painter and medieval window restorer, the source of the heavy black lines characterizing his work. I went into his time as a poverty-stricken painter, and his connection later to Ambrose Vollard, the gallery owner who championed Cezanne and Gauguin. I mentioned his conversion to Catholicism; his paintings of prostitutes, acrobats, circus clowns, and I covered his rise to acceptance, exhibiting with the Fauves and Matisse and designing the décor and costumes for Diaghilev's 1929 ballet *The Prodigal Son*.

I ended with his long and historical legal battle with the Vollard estate, where they insisted on hanging on to some 800 of his paintings, but where Rouault reigned victorious.

When I finished, I waited breathlessly for Professor Hungerland's comments.

After an eternity, he looked directly at me and said, "Very gut, Miss Hoig. But I vunder vy you did not pronounce the artist's name correctly."

Giving the letter 'R' a distinct roll, he stated, "It is 'ROO-OH'. "

Oh no!

Roo-*OH*!

I was flattened, crushed, humiliated!

For days I brooded about my defeat as an art scholar, my disgrace in front of the other students, and my failure to impress Hungerland. I had impressed him in a way, but with my profound ignorance! Evidently my two years of French had had no impact on my brain.

I was somewhat mollified when Hungerland gave me an A- as my overall grade, but I never got over my mortification.

Life went on, and things began to look rosy in other areas.

My pal Farley Sunderson was a character. He had red hair, a wide grin, and was from Spokane. He had fun joking about my hick background. In hindsight, I suppose he might have been gay, but we were a good pair.

Farley was funny. We met in a life drawing class, where we first exchanged glances concerning an overly-hairy female model. She even had hair between her boobs. Later, we cemented our friendship over coffee at the campus diner. Usually it was just the two of us, but sometimes we met in a group.

Farley got his biggest laugh at me one day when the others were discussing a girl student who wore men's ties.

Someone said, "Of course she's a lesbian."

I said, "What's a lesbian?" and Farley almost fell out of his chair laughing.

Although I'd spent time smooching with various and sundry guys over the years, I hadn't had real sex, and was certainly not conversant with the sex practices of others—male, female, or in-between.

I thought about the incident that evening back in my room. At A&M there had been a girl in the dorm, Trixie Van der Pelt, who had been friendly in an overly-demonstrative way—kisses on the mouth, prolonged hugs, etc. I wondered if possibly Trixie, a P.E. major who excelled in sports, was a lesbian. I finally gave up trying to figure it out, and I only hoped that Trixie was happy wherever she was and with whatever she was doing.

Farley knew I was pinching pennies, so he got me a job modeling for the school's evening illustration class. He said they wanted a couple to pose together clothed, and how would I like to earn some extra money posing with him?

The instructor was Paul Carey, whom I learned was co-owner of the art service Logan and Carey in San Francisco. Paul was a small, round-faced Irishman, forever smoking a pipe, and his assistant instructor was a lanky, blue-eyed fellow named Ed Diffenderfer, who worked at Paul's firm. Ed later took over instructing the class alone, since Paul decided he didn't want to spend his evenings teaching.

I thought the young instructor was good-looking, but what a name—*Diffenderfer!* To be saddled with that for a lifetime would be a fate worse than death.

Paul and Ed gradually stopped calling Farley, and I was hired to model alone. Things developed, Ed began to drive me home, and my friendship with Farley faded away.

Sadly, Mark was another connection who evaporated.

After shopping all over Berkeley for the right-sized box, I gave him the cufflinks one Friday night at Al's Steak House on Broadway.

His face lit up. "You made these for me?"

I nodded, holding my breath.

"Well, thank you! They're great! *Beautiful!*"

He put the box away in the pocket of his jacket and began talking to the waiter about our order. The evening ended at the door of my rooming house when Mark said, "I won't be seeing you for a while, sweetie. The folks are taking a trip to Canada and asked me to tag along, so I guess I'll go. Well, *see you!*"

He gave me a passionate kiss, then waved goodbye and drove away.

Something was changing inside me, a change undoubtedly sparked by my new environment. In this new life, my art studies and goal of getting a teaching job were foremost. My brothers had long ago stopped paying attention to our mother's interdictions, so why shouldn't I? I wanted to be a new woman, free of all outdated, old-fangled baggage. Religion no longer seemed a necessary part of my life, but I occasionally visited various Berkeley churches with friend Harriet.

Once I glimpsed Ed Diffenderfer taking up the collection at First Congregational. He nodded to me, and I nodded back and smiled. He asked me out a week later.

At the Claremont Hotel, where Ed took me after a movie (I think it was Jean Renoir's *The River*), he ordered a martini, and when I told him I'd never tasted alcohol, he suggested a frozen daiquiri as my first drink.

It was delicious.

After that, Ed and I went to films often. We saw *From Here to Eternity, Mogambo,* and *Shane,* and we went to foreign films in Berkeley's art cinema houses. *The Red Shoes* and *The Pleasure Garden* were two I remember.

In between movies, we smooched in Ed's Oldsmobile 88 atop wild Grizzly Peak Drive. Once we were rousted by a policeman and told to go home, but Ed said we were just enjoying the view.

Soon I met his parents and in turn, I introduced them to my cousin, her husband, and kids. The geographic connection between our two families made Ed's and my relationship seem inevitable. The Diffenderfer home on Mathieu Avenue was only one street above Fran's house on Crossroads, with tree-lined stairs connecting the two streets.

Ed's family home later burned in the 1991 Oakland fire, but that was long after Mig and George left.

Ever since I'd seen Ed holding the collection plate at the church, I thought he had money, while he assumed that, since I was from Oklahoma, there were oil wells somewhere in my background.

How could we both have been so wrong!

We were engaged for the better part of a year, and when we finally married in July of 1954, my parents came out from Texas and stayed with Fran, Daddy's niece. There wasn't room in my Berkeley apartment, since I had two roommates who refused to leave.

Ed's mother Mig, short for Margaret, was beautiful. She had wavy silver hair, and her posture was tall and stately. I was very fond of her, since she had been so welcoming. After our engagement she took me shopping in San Francisco, and even gave me a formal tea. I had been effusive in my praise of Mig in letters to Mom, and after my parents arrived in California, I sensed jealousy on my mother's part.

"How old is Mig?" she asked.

"I think in her fifties. They had Ed early."

"Humph! A lot can happen to a woman's looks between fifty and sixty!"

Mom wasn't unattractive; she was petite and had a great smile. But she wore her hair pulled back in a severe bun, and ever since her doctor father stated that a woman who wore lipstick looked like a horse's rear end, she refused to wear any makeup. This was despite years of selling powder, rouge, mascara, and lipstick in the drugstore.

I'm afraid my mother looked rather plain and—cursed word—old.

Daddy was charming throughout their visit—didn't seem nearly as nervous as Mother.

"What a wonderful view!" he exclaimed, when Ed's dad drove us in their Chrysler sedan into the Berkeley hills to Grizzly Peak, where you could see both the San Francisco/Oakland Bay bridge and the Golden Gate. Daddy had been to France in World War I as a medic, so was a bit more traveled than my mother, who'd never been anywhere. I remember being pleased that he was so gracious and appreciative with my prospective in-laws.

Now I wonder if he'd exuded all that charm for a reason. I'm pretty sure he didn't pay for the wedding, probably only contributed a small amount.

On one of the hectic days before the ceremony, Daddy took me aside and gave me two pieces of advice.

"After I'm gone, don't let your mother come live with you," was the first.

His second warning was about potential mother-in-law problems. "She's real attached to her son, so watch out!"

The wedding in the Berkeley Congregational Church Chapel was a simple affair, with only family and a few friends invited, which included Ed's Aunt Helen and Uncle Bert Liesy and their two children, 12-year-old Tom and the delightful teenager Barbara. Fran was my matron of honor, and Ed's cousin's husband was best man. I went down the aisle on Daddy's arm wearing a short white satin dress with matching white hat and short veil, all of which I paid for.

Fran looked beautiful, and Mom wore a pretty silvery dress. To please me, she even wore a touch of pink lipstick.

Mig and George gave me a reception. I was in the kitchen where George was slicing tomatoes and muttering, "Next time I get married, I hope it's to a woman who knows how to do something!"

I thought his remark unfair. Mig had sung with the San Francisco Opera Chorus for years, and she was artistically gifted, the source of Ed's talent. Thank God he didn't inherit her fragile nervous system; I didn't know, but Mig had already had one nervous breakdown and was to have another in a few years.

George was an accountant for American Telephone and Telegraph. My father-in-law was one of the most taciturn men I have ever known—a real Silent Sam, but when he finally spoke, you paid attention. Though almost completely bald, he was a handsome man.

When Ed and I arrived at Highland's Inn in Carmel—a wildly popular place for honeymooners—a young male attendant helped us unpack our luggage, and while he was helping me out of the car, my blue wedding garter slipped down to my shoe. Blushing, I stammered, "Uh—*we just got married*." As if he hadn't witnessed something like that a thousand times before.

Ed Diffenderfer *(1928-2023) Diffenderfer's paintings and illustrations have been exhibited in New York, San Francisco, Chicago, Dallas, Los Angeles, and Washington, D.C. His paintings and portraits are in the permanent collection of the Smithsonian Institution, the Pentagon, Library of Congress, National Parks Department, Johnson Space Center in Houston, U.S. Air Force Academy in Colorado, and Lawrence Hall of Science, Berkeley.*

Chapter 7

Bitter Sweet
Noel Coward & Jeanette Macdonald

I had been in California for three years, and had been married for one. I missed my parents and was homesick for the southwest, so we planned a trip to Texas, where I could catch up with my Keever relatives as well.

I finally had a teaching job, but would be off for the summer, and Ed managed to wangle a vacation from the art service.

We planned to go in July. Ed mapped the journey, which would take us over the Sierras to Route 66, near Needles. He chose that route because he'd been to Mammoth Lakes with his parents and wanted to show me the scenery.

We would drive our 1950 Olds 88. It didn't have air-conditioning, so he borrowed a contraption from Paul

Carey that hung on my car window and sprayed cold water. I stayed cool, though slightly damp.

The gizmo conked out somewhere in Arizona, and we both sweltered from then on.

We drove through the Sierras to Mono Lake, a large salty lake formed seven hundred and sixty million years ago, then drove south to Mammoth Lakes, staying the first night in a mountain resort surrounded by snow. My wardrobe didn't stretch that far, so I wore layers.

Ed said we should take US 395 from Mammoth. Later it would connect with 266 S to guide us to Las Vegas.

Somehow, we got lost. Ed blamed me, since I was supposed to keep an eagle eye on the map and tell him where to turn off. I must have been distracted by the air conditioning contraption, which was now spraying yellowish water onto my dress-up clothes on the back seat. We got into a huge argument centering on what a rotten navigator I was. I retorted that he wasn't such a terrific driver, either.

This lasted for twenty miles, until finally, under coercion, he agreed to pull into a gas station, where I got out and asked for directions.

We finally found the right highway, but since it was getting dark we decided to stop at a motel, where all hostilities magically melted away.

The next morning we ate in the nearby diner, accompanied by a horde of burly truck drivers and deranged-looking tourists. Our waitress called me 'Honey' and Ed 'Sweetie', and brought us mouth-watering pancakes and a huge mound of sausages and hash-browns.

The only glitch was the little boy in the next booth who hung over the top and stared at me as I ate.

Once we reached Vegas, we looked for a motel on the Strip. It didn't occur to either of us to gamble. Ed's parents, like mine, were survivors of the Depression, and Ed had learned at his father's knee not to waste money on such things. Although both of my brothers loved to gamble, I never cared to throw money around in such a fashion

Furthermore, Mama had taught me that gambling was a black-hearted sin. Stan and Mel must've missed the lesson.

We investigated the shows, and were delighted to discover that Noel Coward was in town. Gobbling hamburgers and fries, Ed put on a tie, and I wore my going-away outfit, a full-skirted rose taffeta dress and rhinestone earrings. Then we headed for the Desert Inn.

We got lucky, and were led to a table not far from the stage. The room was packed, humming with an excited audience. Coward made his entrance with a full orchestral accompaniment, then stood at the microphone in tuxedo and black suede shoes.

He was thin-lipped and balding, the utmost in suave.

As Coward began to sing, Ed leaned toward me and whispered, "Damn! There's an old trombone buddy of mine in the band! Steve Imbler! We played together years ago in a jumped- up band in Berkeley."

Coward wore a deadpan expression, occasionally smoked, and entertained us for an hour-and-a-half, delivering some of the most sentimental and delightfully funny songs I had ever heard. In a pleasant baritone he crooned his own tunes, starting with a medley: "I'll See You Again," "Dance Little Lady," "A Room With a View," "Someday I'll Find You," and "I'll Follow My Secret Heart."

Then he launched into his signature novelty songs, rolling his R's to a fare-thee-well in "Uncle Harry," "Loch Lomond," "A Bar on the Piccola Marina," and "Mad Dogs and Englishmen."

It was wonderful!

After the show, Ed wanted to go backstage to say hello to his pal Imbler, so even though I was worn out from clapping, I followed him through the curtains. It wasn't easy; we had to tell two different security men why we should be allowed backstage.

Finally, we reached a corridor near a door marked in black letters, NOEL COWARD. Several band members were walking through the hallway, and luckily we ran into Steve right away. While he and Ed had their reunion, I edged toward the star's room. What I was going to do when I got there, I have no idea, but I'd been faced with daunting situations before and had never held back.

Suddenly a large man loomed in front of me. He was probably six feet four, and he had outsized nostrils and bushy black sideburns.

"Where do you think *you're* going?" he asked.

"Uh, nowhere. *Sorry!*"

The door opened, and there stood Mr. Coward.

He gave me a look of frozen animosity that led me to assume he didn't cater to fan support.

"Please get her out of here," he said to Bohunk, "Then get me a very dry martini."

Ed said goodbye to Steve, and we left.

I felt properly chastened, but I had been only a few feet from the mega-star, and he had actually spoken to me, or at least *about* me!

What a triumph!

We checked out early the next morning and decided to have an early breakfast at the Sahara, only a short walk away. The big dining room was nearly deserted; we were the only customers, except for a woman at a booth several paces from where we were sitting.

We ordered, and I said, "Ed! That's Jeanette MacDonald over there!"

What a coincidence! With my expertise in show biz trivia, I knew she'd starred in the movie version of Noel Coward's play *Bitter Sweet*.

Ed looked apprehensive. "It is? For Gosh sakes, don't speak to her, she's enjoying her solitude."

"I'm sure she would love to hear from an admiring fan!"

Ed groaned, but when I finished my eggs, I stood up.

"Wait! What are you going to say?"

"I'll think of something."

I hesitated, then walked over to her booth.

"Miss MacDonald, forgive me, but I have to tell you how much you meant to me when I was growing up. We lived in this windy, dusty little town, but *you* existed in a gorgeous colorful fairyland. I wanted to go there and live a life just like yours. Except I can't sing!"

She smiled and touched her hair, which was no longer a rich auburn but now a faded apricot. Her eyes were still a luminous shade of green, and had opened wide when she saw me approaching.

She tried to reply, but I couldn't shut up.

"My husband and I are passing through on our way to Texas. So, what did you think of the hash browns? Mine tasted a little burnt, but we had some great ones on the way here. What about this *heat!* And have you seen Nelson Eddy lately?"

Miss MacDonald scribbled her name on a napkin and handed it over.

As I walked back to the table, I managed to stumble over a chair. But I didn't mind making a fool of myself when it came to paying homage to an idol of my youth.

Ed paid the check and said, "Promise me you'll never do that again!"

__Noel Coward__ (1899-1973) published more than 50 plays, among them Hay Fever, Private Lives, Design for Living, Present Laughter, and Blithe Spirit. By 1925 Coward had four shows running in the West End: The Vortex, Fallen Angels, Hay Fever and On With the Dance. Coward acted in his own works and others', but collapsed on stage while *starring in an adaptation of* The Constant Nymph. *By 1929 Coward was one of the world's highest-earning writers, with an annual income of £50,000, more than £2,000,000 in today's values. in the 1950s he turned down offers of the roles of the king in the original stage production of* The King and I *and Colonel Nicholson in the film* The Bridge on the River Kwai. *In the same year he turned down the role of Humbert Humbert in* Lolita. *In one of the three plays of* Suite in Three Keys, *(1966)* A Song at Twilight, *Coward at last wrote about homosexuality, playing an explicitly homosexual character. Coward's distinctive clipped diction arose because his mother was deaf; Coward developed his staccato style of speaking to make it easier for her to hear; it also helped eradicate a slight lisp. He was knighted in 1969, and died in Jamaica in 1973. (The Noel Coward Desert Inn show is on YouTube.)*

Jeanette MacDonald *(1903-1965) is best remembered for her musical films of the 1930s with Maurice Chevalier (*The Love Parade, Love Me Tonight, The Merry Widow, One Hour with You*) and Nelson Eddy (*Naughty Marietta, Rose-Marie, Maytime*). During the 30s and 40s, four of her 29 films were nominated for Best Picture Oscars. MacDonald was one of the most influential sopranos of the 20th century, introducing opera to movie audiences and inspiring a generation of singers. Louis B. Mayer promised MacDonald MGM's first Technicolor feature, and made* Sweethearts, *co-*

starring Eddy, in 1938. In 1940, she made Bitter Sweet, a film version of Noel Coward's 1929 stage operetta. Her films were among the top-20 moneymakers in the years they were released, and in Great Britain, from 1937 through 1942, she was one of the top-10 box-office attractions. MacDonald made nightclub appearances, singing and dancing at The Sands and The Sahara in Las Vegas in 1953, and again at The Sahara in 1957. In her later years, she suffered from heart trouble, and in 1963 had an arterial transplant in Houston. She died in 1964 at age sixty-one.

Chapter 8

Okies at the Opera House
Maria Tallchief & George Balanchine

Grand opera was a long tradition in San Francisco and a popular entertainment in the Gold Rush years. San Francisco was "mad for opera" and by 1853 the city had its first resident company. The story goes that the metropolis was trying to keep up with the East in culture and sophistication; also that the melodrama of opera echoed the volatile and violent nature of life during the gold boom.

It wasn't unusual at that time for opera audiences to hiss, yell, and groan during performances, and sometimes fist fights broke out, followed by potential duels.

The Opera Association had its own Chorus School, where members received paid training under company founder Gaetana Merola.

Ed's mother Mig became part of the opera chorus in the 1920's, traveling from Berkeley to the City on the Bay

Bridge. Mig, possessor of a lovely contralto singing voice, was part of the history of operas performed there.

Ed had been to the opera many times with his mother; they had been part of the standing audience for some of the great singers who performed. I had only been to the Opera House to see *The Nutcracker* at Christmas, plus a few times friends or relatives had treated us to tickets.

A year or so after my marriage, Mom flew out to visit. Daddy wasn't well, so she came alone, and Ed and I decided to take her to see *The Firebird* ballet at the Opera House.

It felt good to do something like this for my mother. She had had a life of hard work and privation in the Oklahoma panhandle, which I wrote about in my semi-autobiographical novel *The Wind Came Running*. In that book I emphasized her staunch Scotch-Irish character, her frugality, her strong belief in God, and her struggles to adapt to a man who, more than anything else, loved to hunt quail and raise bird dogs.

Mama hated the dogs. They got loose and ran through her asparagus patch, and the neighbors complained about their constant barking.

I never knew the depths of my mother's longing for me until my own children grew up and moved away. She never gave up the hope that I would move back, and kept urging Ed to apply for a job at one of the Ennis cotton gins.

What *as?* I wondered. An illustrator? An adman? That would be a comedown from the world of San Francisco illustration, and he and I had a good laugh about it.

Some years after leaving, I tried to justify forsaking my home state.

"Mom, there's so much more culture in California!"

"That's ridiculous," she replied.

I think she had no idea of what I was talking about. Either that or she didn't want to acknowledge my argument.

Years went by, and when I complained to Mom that my grown daughter was shunning my company, she said reproachfully, "How about a daughter who leaves and never comes back?"

For the first time, I felt a sense of contrition. Of course, I did go back every summer. But she wanted me with her always, and finally I understood.

Kathleen Keever Hoig was the third child and only daughter of a pioneering horse-and-buggy doctor in Lindsay, Oklahoma, Dr. Adolphus Pinckney Keever. She often accompanied him on his visits to rural patients, and she told me that, as a teenager, she spent a lot of time trying to get patients to pay their bills. She would haggle with them mercilessly, as her father never would, to pay up. With cash; not corn and not bacon.

Mom's most trying times were when my brothers were serving in World War II. They both came through unharmed, but those were difficult years for her.

When I graduated from high school, my parents sold the drugstore in Gage and moved to Fairfax in the north-central part of the state. Daddy found a drugstore where he would be partners with the owner and his hours would be much shorter.

After a lifetime of eating bacon and eggs and smoking a pack of Camels or Lucky Strikes a day, his heart was giving out.

Another reason for the move was that they wanted to be closer to where I would be attending college, only forty miles away, in Stillwater. Stan was already there getting his master's degree in journalism on the GI bill and he could make sure I didn't stray too far from my upbringing.

All of this was something I only realized years later.

In the summer between high school and college, I made friends in my new town. This was Osage County, named for the oil-wealthy Osage Indian tribe, and one of my new friends was a red-haired, freckle-faced girl named Frankie who was unbelievably half-Osage. Frankie was Catholic, and for the first time I attended service in a Catholic church.

It wasn't easy making friends in such a short space of time, but I put my heart and soul into it. So desperate was I to become part of the young Fairfax crowd that one pitch-dark night in a fit of derring-do, I drove them around the cemetery with my headlights off. Two new pals clung to the running boards of our Plymouth sedan, and two more perched on the front fenders. They would have been impressed, except I drove into a deep ditch and barely escaped killing them all. No one was injured, but I don't think the episode made me more popular.

The town's biggest celebrity was Maria Tallchief, who became prima ballerina of the New York City Ballet. Her mother, a petite Caucasian woman, lived up the hill behind my parent's home, and Mom knew her through the drugstore. I think Maria's father, a full-blood Osage, was dead, but he may have been living elsewhere.

The Osage Nation of Oklahoma has retained collective ownership of the mineral rights to all of Osage County through treaties, and their oil rights made the tribe one of the wealthiest groups of people in the world. That was how Maria and Marjorie, who also became a ballerina, got their dance training in Oklahoma City.

Before the performance, as we walked through the opera house's imposing corridors with its towering ceilings, Mom said, "Maybe we'll see Mrs. Tallchief!"

I replied in my newly acquired, world-weary tones, "Mo—*ther!* This is California!"

We turned the corner, and there was Mrs. Tallchief!

After our greetings, she said, "After the performance, why don't you go backstage and say hello to Maria?"

To my surprise Ed said, "Maybe we will!"

The house was packed, and Maria's performance to Tchaikovsky's immortal music was thrilling.

It was an unforgettable night, and we did go backstage. We never got to meet Maria, but her choreographer husband, George Balanchine, came to the dressing room door. When we explained that Maria's mother was Mom's neighbor in Oklahoma, he was warm and gracious, but said, "Maria izz a little tired. I will tell her that you from hometown were here."

His accent was unmistakable, and I opened my mouth to ask, "Do you miss Russia?" intending to follow up with a question about his impressions of American culture. Mom appeared eager to make his acquaintance; she was someone who, if the occasion arose, could have conversed for hours with Haile Selassie or Mao Zedong.

Before either of us could start a conversation, Ed took us by the arm and led us away.

I didn't know then that Maria and Balanchine had been divorced for some time, and that he was now married to his latest prima ballerina, Tanaquil LeClercq. Did that information spoil my memories of that unbelievable night, first seeing *Firebird*, then meeting Maria's famous dance master?

No.

The memory lingers on, and now, if I'm lucky enough to attend a performance at the opera house, I close my eyes and remember that fantastic night.

In the car on the way home, I asked Mom if she'd enjoyed herself, and she said, "Oh, very much! I can't wait to tell Ed and Gladys about it when I get home!"

Then she muttered, "But they'll just try to top me—talkin' about some hifalutin party they went to in Dallas."

Maria Tallchief (1925-2013) was the definitive American ballerina of the 1940's and '50s. She was wife and muse to the 20th century's master choreographer George Balanchine, and leading ballerina of New York City Ballet. She became a partner to both Rudolf Nureyev and Erik Bruhn, as well as the lover of both. Tall and long-legged, with the darkly aquiline looks of her father, Alexander Tall Chief, she set a standard for speed and expressiveness. Tallchief, born in Fairfax, Oklahoma, was one of three children of Alexander and Ruth Tall Chief. Her younger sister Marjorie also became a ballerina. Home was the Osage reservation on which oil was plentiful, making her family wealthy. Her father was the grandson of Chief Bigheart Tall Chief, who led negotiations with the U.S. government on behalf of the Osage tribe over oil revenues. Her mother was from a Scots-Irish immigrant family.

In 1942, aged 17, Maria began her career with Ballet Russe de Monte Carlo. Choreographer George Balanchine joined the troupe, and Tallchief became his third wife in 1946. Among the many ballets of Balanchine's on which she stamped her technical brilliance were Orpheus, The Firebird, Scotch Symphony, Allegro Brilliante and his versions of Swan Lake and The Nutcracker. Tallchief and Balanchine divorced amicably, and the choreographer continued to create ballets for her. Her marriage to third husband Henry Paschen lasted 48 years, surviving Maria's affairs with her celebrated partners, Erik Bruhn and Rudolf Nureyev. She is survived by her daughter, poet Elise Paschen, and her sister, the former ballerina Marjorie Tallchief.

George Balanchine *(1904-1983) was born Giorgi Melitonovitch Balanchivadze in Saint Petersburg, Russia. In 1913 he was accepted into the Imperial Ballet School. While still in his teens, Balanchine choreographed his first work, a pas de deux named* La Nuit, *followed by another duet,* Enigma, *with the dancers in bare feet. On a 1924 visit to Germany with the Soviet State Dancers, Balanchine, his wife Tama Geva, and other dancers fled to Paris, where there was a large Russian community. Impresario Sergei Diaghilev invited Balanchine to join the Ballets Russes as a choreographer, promoting him to Ballet Master. Between 1924 and Diaghilev's death in 1929, Balanchine created nine ballets, as well as lesser works. He worked with composers Sergei Prokofiev, Igor Stravinsky, Claude Debussy, Erik Satie, and Maurice Ravel, and with artists who designed sets and costumes, Picasso, Rouault, and Matisse. In 1931, the Ballet Russe de Monte Carlo was hired Leonide Massine and Balanchine as choreographers. Balanchine created new works, including collaborations with composers Kurt Weill, Darius Milhaud, Henri Sauguet, and designer Pavel Tchelitchew.*

Balanchine came to the U.S. in 1934. The School of American Ballet opened to students less than 3 months after Balanchine arrived, a home for dancers of New York City ballet and companies from all over the world. Balanchine choreographed for musical theater with Richard Rodgers, Lorenz Hart, and Vernon Duke. He choreographed Broadway's On Your Toes, featuring the ballet Slaughter On Tenth Avenue. Balanchine moved his company to Hollywood and created dances for five movies, all of which featured Vera Zorina, who became his third wife. New York City offered his company residency; in 1955 he created his version of The Nutcracker, in which he played Drosselmeyer. Other famous Balanchine ballets created with the company are Firebird, Allegro Brilliante, Agon, The Seven Deadly Sins, and Episodes. In 1967, Balanchine created the ballet Jewels.

In 1923 in Russia, Balanchine married Tamara Geva, a sixteen-year-old dancer. They divorced, and later he married and divorced three more times, all to women who were his dancers: Vera Zorina, Maria Tallchief, and Tanaquil LeClerq. Balanchine died in 1983, aged 79. He had a Russian Orthodox funeral, and was interred in a cemetery in Sag Harbor, New York.

Chapter 9

Honest and Plainspoken Maurice Logan

I remember we were late getting up that Saturday because we'd had to call the plumber in the middle of the night. One of the toilets was leaking water and wouldn't stop.

Then after we finally got to bed, a neighbor called and woke me up around 9:30. It was Rosemary next door, who was always running out of things, and wanted to borrow two eggs. When the doorbell rang, I went to the door in my robe, hair tousled and uncombed, holding the eggs in my hand.

But it wasn't Rosemary, it was Maurice Logan, Ed's boss along with Paul Carey at the art service. I let him in and rushed to get Ed out of bed.

"Get up! Mr. Logan is here! Wasn't he supposed to come at eleven?"

"Oh God!" Ed said, sitting up in bed. "Has the toilet stopped running?"

"Never mind that. Get up!"

It wasn't as if we hadn't prepared for Mr. Logan's visit. The day before, Ed raked the yard, and I baked a pound cake which unfortunately ended up burnt on the bottom. It looked fine on top, though.

We got dressed and, apologizing profusely while explaining the plumbing crisis, managed to get our guest seated.

Now a new embarrassment came along.

We'd acquired a beagle puppy, Shammy, named because her ears were as soft as chamois-skin. Shammy was our first child, and anything she did, save chewing up our sweaters and oil paints (alizarin crimson was her favorite) and defecating in forbidden spots, amused and entertained us.

That morning she must have sensed our excitement about our guest, and she raced like a rocket from her end of the house to the living room, where she jumped into the lap of Mr. Logan!

We were relieved when he laughed, so we laughed too. It pleased Ed to see this tall, distinguished-looking gentleman enjoying our puppy.

Maurice Logan was a highly respected Bay Area artist, co-founder of one of San Francisco's early art services, Logan, Staniford and Carey. He and his wife lived only a few miles from us, and Ed had invited him over to see our house. He was interested because he was a friend of the former owner, Hamilton Wolf, a teaching colleague at CCAC. Wolf had built the house hiring Campbell and Wong, up-and-coming architects of the period. He had to sell it because of his wife's bad health.

Maury is famous now because he was a member of the Society of Six, a group of early California outdoor painters who banded together to sketch and paint. Besides Logan, the group included William Clapp, Seldon Gile, August Gay, Bernard Von Eichman, and Louis Siegriest. Several were members of the Bohemian Club, and there is a large portrait of Logan painted by illustrator Lonnie Bee just inside the front door of the city club. Logan is wearing a painter's smock over his suit and tie. Those were the days of dignity in dress, even among artists.

My hands shook as I poured coffee and sliced burnt pound cake. To Ed, Maury was not just a boss, he was a mentor who helped to jump-start his career. He also sponsored him for the Bohemian Club.

Mr. Logan and I had met before, but in case he'd forgotten, I strived to make a good impression. The man was already an icon. But Ed had told me that he was down-to-earth and plainspoken, which was a big relief. The Keevers and Hoigs were noted for their plain speech and unadorned style.

While sipping coffee and gazing out the window at our blooming tea trees, Mr. Logan remarked, "Lovely home! Have you two been enjoying yourselves here?"

Ed and I were typical young newlyweds, delighting in one another in every way, including sexually. Striving for forthrightness, I said, "Oh yes, especially in the bedroom!"

Mr. Logan looked a little shocked, so I backtracked.

"I mean—we have breakfast there, and the doggie bed is there. Sometimes we play games in bed. Checkers or rummy."

I made a broad gesture with my hands. "My mother wouldn't approve of any of it—especially having our dog in the bedroom!"

I didn't know how I'd stumbled so far off track, but I blathered on. "She disapproves of our—I mean Mom's very churchy—you know, church-oriented!"

My face felt hot.

Mr. Logan had stopped looking at me and was staring at the rug.

Finally Ed, whose face was probably even redder than mine, rescued me. "Honey, would you mind getting more coffee?"

Sighing with relief, I sprinted for the kitchen.

It was hours later when Rosemary finally showed up to get the eggs.

Mr. Logan continued to paint and sketch outdoors until his death at ninety-one. We have one of his watercolors, which he gave us not long after his visit. I took it as a sign that he didn't hold my conversation against me.

Either that, or he wanted to show his sympathy for Ed.

Maurice Logan (1886-1977) was born in San Francisco and studied at the Mark Hopkins Institute of Art (San Francisco), California College of Arts and Crafts (Oakland) and Chicago Art Institute. He was a member of the National Academy of Design, American Watercolor Society, and California Water Color Society. By the mid '20s, he was one of San Francisco's best known commercial illustrators and poster designers. During this era, he produced colorful expressionist oil paintings and exhibited as a member of the Society of Six. In the 1930's, he helped form the Thirteen Watercolorists group. In 1924 he was sent on expedition to British East Africa, Kenya, to make sketches for dioramas to be used in the Los Angeles Museum of History, Science and Art.

He was known for his Sunset and Westways magazine covers and many advertising posters. His art agency had a list of lucrative accounts: Dole, Lucky Lager Beer, Ghirardelli Chocolate, and Standard Oil of California.

He won many prizes, and in 1957 had a one-man show at the de Young Museum in San Francisco. As an art instructor in Oakland, Logan was on the board of directors of the Society of Western Artists, the West Coast Watercolor Society and other art clubs. He juried art exhibitions at the Oakland Art Museum and was a member of the Bohemian Club.

Chapter 10

Backstage Sage
Melvyn Douglas & Helen Gahagan Douglas

You never forget someone who is famous, humble, and gracious, and I'll never forget Melvyn Douglas.

Before we had children, and when I was teaching, Ed and I were able to treat ourselves to all sorts of nice things. We went on short auto trips, dined out once a week, and went to the theater several times a year. We loved the Geary theater, and the plays we wanted to see appeared there. It's a theater with a good deal of history, rising from the rubble of the 1906 earthquake. Then, when the 1989 Loma Prieta earthquake tore a huge hole in the ceiling, destroying the proscenium arch and dumping tons of debris on the first six rows of seats, the theater community raised $30 million to rebuild, and it was up and running within a couple of years.

In 1956, *Inherit the Wind* came to the Geary with Melvyn Douglas as the Clarence Darrow character, and we eagerly bought tickets. This was a courtroom drama about the fight against teaching evolution in the public schools. In 1925, in Tennessee, a substitute high school teacher, John T. Scopes, was accused of violating the state's Butler Act, which had made it unlawful to teach human evolution in state-funded schools. The ACLU staged the trial to attract publicity. Scopes was found guilty and fined $100, and now everyone in the country knew about this issue.

I had been a fan of Douglas's for a long time. Through the years I had made sporadic trips into Berkeley's art movie houses to see Ernst Lubitsch's *Ninotchka*, where Douglas not only romanced Garbo but was able to make her laugh. I laughed, too, at seeing the dour Communist Garbo buy a silly hat and drink champagne.

Inherit the Wind, set entirely in the courtroom, was amazingly intense. Our experience with Balanchine a few years before had emboldened us, so Ed and I went backstage to congratulate Douglas on his amazing characterization. The tall, handsome actor not only came to the door of his dressing room, he introduced us to his wife, Helen Gahagan Douglas, who sat in the semi-dark smiling in our direction.

We praised the play and his acting, and he said, "It's important that young people like you see this play! I'm very glad you came."

We went away feeling as if we had represented our generation in some grand achievement. On the drive home,

I recalled what I remembered about his wife, that she had run as a Democrat against Richard Nixon for the Senate in 1950, and that while campaigning he'd called her "pink right down to her underwear."

"And she's the one who first called him "Tricky Dicky, remember?" said Ed.

When Mr. Douglas won the Oscar for *Hud*, a role which evoked every old rancher I'd ever known back home, we were delighted. We saw all of his movie and television performances, and years later, when our son decided to become an actor, we couldn't have been more pleased.

> ***Melvyn Douglas*** *(1901-1981) was one of America's finest actors. In addition to two Oscars, he also won a Tony Award and an Emmy. On Broadway, in Tonight or Never, Douglas met the woman who would be his wife of 50 years, his co-star Helen Gahagan. Douglas was a great liberal and pillar of the anti-Nazi Popular Front in Hollywood of the '30s. A supporter of President Franklin Roosevelt, Douglas' leftism would come back to haunt him after the death of FDR. He was active in politics and one of the leading lights of the anti-Communist left in the late '30s and early '40s. He, along with fellow liberals Edward G. Robinson and Henry Fonda, were "gray listed" (not blacklisted, they just weren't offered any work). The late '40s brought the blacklist to Hollywood, after the HUAC grilling of the Hollywood help led to the exposure and persecution of the Hollywood 10.*

After appearing in six films as a leading man and second lead in A-List pictures, 1947-49, Douglas made just two films in the 1950's, supporting roles at RKO in 1951, until he reappeared later in Peter Ustinov's Billy Budd. In the '50s Douglas starred in Playhouse 90. He made many appearances on Broadway in the '40s and '50s, winning a Tony for his lead role in the 1960 play The Best Man by Gore Vidal. For his second role after coming off the gray list, he won Best Supporting Actor Oscar as Paul Newman's father in Hud. Other films were Chayefsky's The Americanization of Emily, CBS Playhouse's Do Not Go Gentle Into That Good Night, for which he won a Best Actor Emmy, and was in The Candidate as Robert Redford's father. For his performance in I Never Sang for My Father, Douglas got his sole Best Actor Academy Award nod.

He had a career renaissance in the late 1970's, appearing in The Seduction of Joe Tynan, Being There, and Ghost Story, winning his second Oscar for Being There. In 1967, he became the fifth performer to win the triple crown of acting. Oscar: Best Supporting Actor, Hud, and Best Supporting Actor, Being There, Tony: Best Actor-Play, The Best Man (1960) and Emmy: Best Actor-Drama, CBS Playhouse: Do Not Go Gentle Into That Good Night. He won Broadway's 1960 Tony Award as Best Actor for The Best Man.

Helen Gahagan Douglas (1900-1980) Broadway singer and actress, appeared in only one film, portraying the title character in H. Rider Haggard's She in 1935. In 1950 Douglas ran as a Democrat for the U.S. Senate and was opposed by the Republican nominee, red-baiting candidate Richard Nixon, who charged her with being soft on Communism due to her opposition to HUAC and her stance insisting that the U.S. improve its relations with the USSR. Nixon tarred her as a fellow traveler of Communists, a pinko who was "pink right down to her underwear." But it was Douglas who gave Nixon his most famous nickname, "Tricky Dicky." While historians have written that she was defeated by Nixon because of his unethical behavior and dirty campaign tactics, her pro-Soviet, anti-Cold War stance had alienated President Truman, who refused to campaign for her. President Kennedy appointed her Treasurer of the United States in 1961.

During a period when Jim Crow laws still applied in the nation's capital, Helen Douglas used her status to challenge prevailing racial attitudes. The first white Representative with African Americans on her staff, she also sought to desegregate Capitol restaurants. Douglas's role as a spokesperson for liberal causes made her beloved by liberals and reviled by conservatives. In October 1945, Douglas lashed out at the House Un–American Activities Committee, which was investigating alleged communist sympathizers and focused on many Hollywood writers and artists. Douglas argued that this was unconstitutional, and critics charged that she was a communist fellow traveler.

Chapter 11

Swimming to Belvedere
Russell Nype

Ed and I were invited to yet another music party, this time in Marin County. It was Sunday, August 5, 1962, and the reason we were invited was because of Ed's talent on the trombone. He played with a large band as well as a smaller jazz group in the Bohemian Club, and we were invited to many social gatherings because he was part of the entertainment.

I was a more-than-willing participant. I had learned how to drink and smoke, and I loved people and parties.

Belvedere is a beautiful and elegant enclave in Marin, where every home is on a hill with a smashing view of San Francisco Bay. Not only did this house have the most eye-popping vista I'd ever seen, it also had a swimming pool.

We'd heard that it once belonged to illustrator John Falter of *Saturday Evening Post* fame, and possibly was built by him. Falter did more than a hundred covers for the *Post*, plus illustrations for numerous other magazines. He had moved from the Bay Area some time ago. As a young illustrator, my husband admired Falter's work, so he was anxious to see the house. Not only that, he had once met Falter at the Bohemian Grove, and the two of them had circled around to various camps, Ed playing his horn and Falter accompanying him on piano.

Our host and hostess were a charming, extroverted couple who immediately made us feel welcome. I learned later that Merritt Ruddock was an ex-mayor of Belvedere, as well as present director of the World Affairs Council of Northern California.

These folks were *connected*.

There were a few celebrities at the party: Bishop Pike, the flamboyant Episcopal priest from Grace Cathedral on Nob Hill, plus a cluster of socialites I'd glimpsed on the Society pages of the *Chronicle*. There was also a musical comedy star, Russell Nype, currently appearing in San Francisco in *Hello Dolly!* with Elaine Stritch.

I was sitting with my pal Charlotte Martens when the Bishop walked past in his purple vest, black tunic, and gold chain with its large gold cross.

"Well! If I'd known it was going to be a costume party . . . " she remarked, and I burst out laughing.

Ed and I didn't go to the theater now; our budget was stretched for house payments, car payments, and children, so we hadn't seen the show.

Couples were already dancing in a large cleared area in the main room. While Ed joined the other musicians, I started dancing with anyone who asked me. With two babies at home aged one and three, I was delighted to be here, mingling with the world.

The music got louder and wilder, and it wasn't long before I had taken off my shoes and was whirling around the floor.

It was a day for parading one's wares. Bishop Pike displayed his purple tunic and gold chains, the musicians strutted their stuff, and I flaunted my new yellow dress with its flaring skirt. Was this how a young mother and former schoolteacher should behave? Of course not! But I knew Ed didn't mind as long as he got to play his music. I could have balanced a lampshade on my head or turned somersaults in the center of the room, and he would have continued to glide his trombone slide without noticing.

The party came to an end around one o'clock in the morning. Both of us had had a great time, so great that when I left, I forgot to take my shoes.

Over breakfast in my customary morning-after remorseful state, I asked myself, *Why did I behave like that? Why did I drink so much?* I dimly recalled pulling someone else's husband onto the floor to dance and also had a blurred memory of twirling around like a top—*solo!*

Why was I even born?

When I called Marge Ruddock around ten o'clock that morning and said I'd left my shoes, she said, "Come over and get them, darling, and we'll all go swimming!"

I felt reassured. Maybe I hadn't disgraced myself after all.

I had a wonderful arrangement with Mrs. Williams next door. An elderly woman, wife of the caretaker for the big Spanish house our modest home sat next to, she absolutely loved our babies. I had driven Ed to the bus that morning, so after Marge gave me detailed driving directions and Mrs. WIlliams said she could baby-sit, I drove across the San Rafael bridge to Belvedere.

Marge welcomed me with open arms, and I changed into my new blue swimsuit, then walked down a long stretch of stairs to the pool. After having my children, I no longer had my former shape, but thankfully had shopped for a new suit with built-in tummy control.

When I stepped into the water, there was Russell Nype.

He and Merritt were treading water and talking about the Giants. I gathered that Willie Mays, Orlando Cepeda, and Felipe Alou had led the team in a great winning streak, and I heard the words 'National League title' and 'beat the Dodgers!'

After a lap or two, I swam to the side of the pool, got out, and asked the white-coated waiter for a Bloody Mary. Feeling hungover, I sat down at a poolside table, and by the time I'd finished my drink, the place had regained some of its glamour of the day before. The sky was now bluer, the water a brighter aqua. My skin felt deliciously damp, and I began to feel more self-confident, even chirpy.

Our host and hostess had gone off somewhere, and Mr. Nype got out of the pool and joined me in his first Bloody Mary and my second. He began to ask questions about my teaching career, where we lived, was my husband a professional musician, etc.

I asked, "Are you enjoying performing in San Francisco?"

"Yes, the audiences are wonderful! But I'm glad to get away for a break like this."

He had a pleasing baritone voice.

Well, *duh!*

He leaned toward me to light my cigarette, smiling and rather flirtatious.

I kept worrying about the night before. Had he noticed that I'd behaved like a manic floozy? I searched his eyes for signs of repulsion, but saw none.

I then began offering up a load of vodka-fueled idiotic chatter.

"What's Elaine Stritch like? I like to act, too! I was in a play in high school where I had to say, 'You have grasped the idea in its entirety.'"

Mr. Nype let me blather on, nodding and encouraging me to talk. But I needed no encouragement. The topper I came up with was, "I suppose you must get romantically involved with all of your co-stars?" a question he had the good sense not to answer.

We landed on the sad topic of Marilyn Monroe's suicide, which we'd all learned about the day before. Ed and I had heard about it as we stood admiring the view with other guests. I remember the hush that came over the group, and how no one spoke for several seconds.

Then we began asking, *How did she do it? Why did she do it?*—the same questions still being asked today.

I asked Russell whether he had ever worked with her. He said no, but that he knew some actors who'd met Monroe at the Actors Studio in New York.

"What did they think of her talent?"

"Half of them thought she was great, and the other half thought she was in over her head."

Marge called down from above that she was serving lunch, but I said I had to leave. I grabbed my towel and Russell and I climbed the stairs together.

Back in the house, I mentioned that I had two little ones at home. "I have to get back to reality. But you've all been so kind. I feel as if I've been on vacation!"

I changed clothes, and as I walked out the door clasping my wet swimsuit and party shoes, I shook Russell's hand.

"It's been a pleasure!" he said, pressing my fingers longer than necessary.

Driving home, and praying that I wouldn't get stopped by the Highway Patrol, I wondered why I had been so stage-struck. The actor had been super-friendly, and I wondered if the situation had been different, could a romance have blossomed?

In the end I decided that even if he was flirting, it was probably nothing more than good manners.

Not long ago I came across Russell Nype and Ethel Merman on YouTube singing Irving Berlin's "You're Just in Love" from *Call Me Madam*. There's a second version, with Nype and Elaine Stritch singing the same song. Merman is better than Stritch by a country mile, but Russell sounds the same in both videos. Except in the later one he has white hair.

> **Russell Nype** *(1920-2018) was born in Zion, Illinois, an American actor and singer. He made his Broadway debut in the opera Regina in 1949. The following year he won critical acclaim and both the Tony and Theatre World Awards for his performance opposite Ethel Merman in Call Me Madam. The two were reunited in 1970 when in the run of the original production of Hello, Dolly! Merman joined the show in the title role and Nype was cast as Cornelius Hackl. Nype appeared in revivals of Carousel, Brigadoon, and Mornings at Seven, and opposite Elaine Stitch in Goldilocks, for which he won his second Tony. Nype's feature film credits include Love Story, Can't Stop the Music, and The Stuff. On television he appeared in Studio One, Fantasy Island, One Day at a Time, The Cosby Show, Murder, She Wrote, Who's the Boss? and productions of One Touch of Venus, Kiss Me, Kate and Mornings at Seven.*

Bishop James Albert Pike *(1913-1969) was an American Episcopal, accused heretic, writer, and one of the first mainline religious figures to appear regularly on television. Pike's outspoken and heretical views on many theological and social issues made him one of the most controversial public figures of his time. He was an early proponent of the ordination of women and racial desegregation within mainline churches. Pike was the fifth Bishop of California.*

His episcopate was marked by both professional and personal controversy. While at Grace Cathedral he was involved with promoting a living wage for workers in San Francisco, the acceptance of LGBT people in the church, and civil rights. Later he ordained a woman as a first-order deacon, now known as a "transitional deacon," usually the first step in the process towards ordination in the priesthood in the Episcopal church. The ordination was not approved until after Pike's death. Among his notable accomplishments, Pike invited Martin Luther King, Jr. to speak at Grace Cathedral in San Francisco in 1965 following his march to Selma, Alabama.

Chapter 12

Cow Palace Pols
William Scranton

That July of 1964, I probably shouldn't have been traipsing off to the Republican Convention. My children were very young and didn't like me to leave, and I wasn't even a Republican, for gosh sakes! But the media had been full of the convention and the famous political figures attending, and it was being held just across the bay at the Cow Palace in Daly City.

My cousin Fran was having serious marital problems, Ed had left for the Grove encampment on the Russian River, and I was longing for a taste of freedom from childcare, washing machines, and responsibility.

By now Fran and I were not just first cousins, but best friends. She had several close pals among the other Oakland doctors' wives, but she seemed to have room in her life for me as well. I think she enjoyed helping me, or maybe she felt that I, ten years younger, was herself in a younger incarnation. Also, she could confide in me more easily than the wives of her own social set. Fran had the social standing and comfortable lifestyle afforded to doctors' wives, but was tied down with four children and a husband who loved dominos and golf. We'd begun to spend a lot of time together, so it wasn't surprising when she called and asked, "Want to go to the convention? I'll drive."

"Sure!" I said. I hurried next door and asked Mrs. Williams to babysit, and she said she could.

On that first morning of the convention, since we'd heard that all the candidates were staying there, we drove to the Mark Hopkins hotel in San Francisco. There was minimum security, and we were in the lobby when President Eisenhower came through—flashbulbs popping, excited press milling around him and his entourage. We had heard that he supported Rockefeller as his successor.

When the flurry of excitement was over, we ordered an early lunch at the hotel, then began to discuss our marriages. My troubles were miniscule compared to hers.

Ed had so much more freedom than I did! He was away for many weekends at his club encampment in the summer, and he also went on occasional trips for the Air Force, who sent artists all over the world to illustrate their outreach. During those years, Ed took Air Force-sponsored trips to Japan and Cape Canaveral, donating paintings to the USAF art collection. (The collection is now housed at the Pentagon and the Air Force Academy in Colorado Springs.)

On the other hand, my freedom was severely curtailed when we started our family. I had wanted children, but now was stuck at home. I needed more attention from him, and more emotional support raising our kids.

One worry concerned our little daughter Katy, a thumb-sucker. I worried constantly about how I could help her, and, concerned about future dental problems, tried lots of remedies, the latest being a nasty-tasting liquid applied to her thumb at bedtime.

This made her start wetting the bed, so now we had two problems instead of one. Three, if you count my lost sleep changing her sheets. Maybe the solution was getting a kitten. She had asked for one, and I had almost decided to do it, even though Ed said he hated cats. He preferred dogs, and we already had Shammy the beagle.

He added that if I got a cat it would be over his dead body.

The Cow Palace Pavilion is situated north of San Francisco, a huge event facility with multiple buildings. Completed in 1941, it hosted the San Francisco Warriors from 1962 to 1964, and again from 1966 to 1971.

The idea for the arena was inspired by the popularity of the livestock pavilion at the 1915 Panama-Pacific International Exposition. A local newspaper asked in May,

1935, "Why, when people are starving, should money be spent on a 'palace for cows'? A headline writer turned the phrase around, ending with the name 'Cow Palace'.

When we finally arrived at the vast parking lot, we were accosted by a young man who asked, "Would you ladies like to march into the convention as Scranton supporters?"

We had no idea who Scranton was, but there was a group already gathered near the entrance carrying signs that proclaimed *SCRANTON FOR PRESIDENT*. We nodded in unison.

In for a penny, in for a pound.

He handed us placards mounted on tall poles, and we joined the group of twenty or so. Our group, a ragtag collection of tall and short, old and young citizens who looked as if we'd been thrown together on short notice, which we had, began to promenade into the immense smoke-filled hall. Governor Scranton joined us, a medium-tall man wearing a medium-brown suit with a medium-handsome face. His feeble smile communicated little confidence in this endeavor, and he didn't utter a word.

We marched in and out of the aisles of chairs, then in front of the high stage, where Nelson Rockefeller stood at a podium poised to make a speech.

Fran and I responded immediately to the excitement of the place. The floor was swarming with bodies, manic conventioneers roaming about wearing crazy hats. *And look!* There's Roger Mudd, wearing a gigantic, burdensome TV contraption on his back.

And over there, Eric Sevareid! And *look*, look to your right! Huntley, with Brinkley!

When our group of supporters began to scatter, Fran and I were approached by a young reporter wearing a porkpie hat.

"I'm from the *San Jose Mercury*," he said. "Would you ladies mind answering some questions?"

"Okay," I said. "Fire ahead!"

"Why were you marching for Scranton? What are the tenets of his platform which you support?"

We were feeling the wine we'd imbibed at lunch, and also were intoxicated by the whipped-up crowd.

"We didn't have anything else to do, so we thought—why not?" said Fran, giggling.

I added, "We never heard of the guy until a few minutes ago!"

The reporter frowned, clutching his pad to his chest. He stood there for a long moment, then hurried away. Evidently our irreverent approach to politics was not what he wanted to write about.

We went into gales of laughter and started climbing the steps leading to the upper reaches of the auditorium, where we could get a bird's-eye view. We climbed up, then climbed up some more, and finally sat down. There were very few people sitting up this high, but I noticed that Senator John Tower from Texas was perched just a few feet away. I wondered why he'd positioned himself so far from the action. I recalled that he was a super-conservative and probably backing Goldwater, but that didn't explain why he was planted up here in the clouds.

Finally, Rockefeller began to speak, and to our amazement, the building suddenly echoed with loud boos. The raucous catcalls went on and on, and the Goldwater delegates eventually drowned him out.

Speech after boring speech followed, and an hour later, Fran and I decided to leave. The drive home seemed to take forever. We were exhausted, and didn't go back after that.

That night, in one of my crazy dreams, I was floating in the air inside the Cow Palace, and the huge crowd was looking up and trying to get me to come down. They yelled that Eric Sevareid wanted to interview me about who I thought was going to get the nomination for president.

But I wouldn't come down. I didn't know the answer and didn't want them to find out.

I woke up when I heard Katy calling.

"Mommy! Mommy!"

I got out of bed and went to go change her sheets.

On the last day of the convention the final balloting for president was: Barry Goldwater, 883; William Scranton, 214; Nelson Rockefeller, 114; George Romney, 41; Margaret Chase Smith, 27; Walter Judd, 22; Hiram Fong, 5; Henry Cabot Lodge, Jr., 2.

I called Fran, "Can you believe it? Our guy came in second!"

In November we were delighted when Goldwater was defeated by Lyndon Johnson. With 61%, Johnson won the highest share of the popular vote of any candidate since James Monroe ran unopposed in 1820.

The morning after I marched for Scranton, Katy and I answered an ad for free kittens, then went out and brought home a sweet orange-and-white fuzz ball. We named her 'Punkin,' and miraculously, Ed didn't keel over and die. Instead, he fell in love with the furry little thing.

Punkin liked to play and nap, play and nap, as kittens do. I had worried that our beagle wouldn't accept a new member of the household, but they developed an amicably wary relationship, and their skirmishes entertained us all day long.

I don't remember how long it took for Katy to stop sucking her thumb after we got Punkin, but finally, she did.

William Scranton (1917–2013) an American Republican Party politician and diplomat, served as the 38th Governor of Pennsylvania from 1963 to 1967. Born into the prominent Scranton family, he graduated from Yale Law School and served in the United States Army Air Corps during World War II. After the war, he practiced law and became active in the Pennsylvania Republican Party, won election to the U.S. House of

Representatives in 1960, and gained a reputation as a moderate in Congress. He won the Republican nomination in Pennsylvania's 1962 gubernatorial election, defeating a democrat in the general election.

As governor, Scranton presided over sweeping reforms to Pennsylvania education, including the creation of the state's community college system. Scranton entered the race for the 1964 Republican presidential nomination after the collapse of Nelson Rockefeller's candidacy, but Barry Goldwater won the nomination. Scranton went out of office in 1967 but remained active in politics, serving as a member of the transition team for President Gerald Ford, and later as U.S. Ambassador to the United Nations (1976-1977).

Chapter 13

Eagle In One
Charles Schulz & Dale Robertson

In the mid-'60s, Oakland had no live theater. Next door, the Berkeley theater was well established, but we Oaklanders wanted something of our own. An organization called the Oakland Repertory Guild was formed, and I was asked to join. I loved theater and wanted to help promote it, so why not? The organization promised to be very social, with a Christmas party where the men donned tuxes and the ladies got equally gussied up.

We put on preview events to raise money to build a theater, along with other fundraisers, and we sponsored quite a few important plays. In 1966 we imported Mildred Dunnock, John Saxon, and Yvette Mimeux from Hollywood to do *The Glass Menagerie*. Soon after that, Peter Cook and Dudley Moore performed for us their hit satire *Beyond the Fringe*.

One September, because someone thought we had a tangential connection to show business, we Guild members were asked to be hostesses at a celebrity golf tournament, a benefit for Oakland's Children's Hospital. All we had to do was be charming and welcome the golfers to Oakland, and my pal Colleen Brooks and I said we would love to do it. We drove out to Sequoyah Country Club near Knowland Park for the cocktail party, held on the eve of the tournament. We slowed our car to admire the Spanish style clubhouse set among towering pines and redwoods, then parked and walked in.

We ordered wine from the bar and joined the noisy throng in a huge reception room. One of the first celebrities I spotted was Dale Robertson. Recalling the many other actors from my home state, from Will Rogers to Ben Johnson, Dennis Weaver, and James Garner, I decided to greet him first.

I was pretty sure I looked good. I was wearing a new lime-green jumpsuit, dangling silver earrings, and thin-strapped high heels.

"Hi, how are you, Mr. Robertson? I'm from Oklahoma, too!"

"Is that right?" he said, then turned his back and began to chat with another golfer.

H-m-m-m-m, I thought.

Maybe he doesn't want to be reminded of where he's from. No, that couldn't be it; I'd read that he still had a ranch near Oklahoma City. I learned later that Robertson had been married four times, so maybe he was leery of women. Or maybe he came to the tournament to play golf, not be annoyed by someone who acted like an aggressive fan.

I walked over to where Colleen was scintillating Clint Eastwood, and when Clint was accosted by another golfer, I asked her, "Incidentally, do you know anything about golf?"

"Not a friggin' thing," she said.

Colleen was gorgeous; tall, raven-haired, with big eyes accentuated by heavy makeup. She was also very brainy and funny, and her satires had been published in *The New Yorker*.

We got refills on wine, then strolled around the room, stopping when we encountered the cartoonist Charles Schulz. He was standing in front of a floor-to-ceiling window overlooking the golf course, looking rumpled and slightly uncomfortable.

All at once I became tongue-tied. Being rebuffed by Robertson had temporarily silenced me, and here was a man with immense talent who was world-famous! *Peanuts* was in worldwide distribution in hundreds of foreign languages, and *A Charlie Brown Christma*s had recently won an Emmy. My kids loved it!

I'd seen a television interview in which Schulz admitted that, like Charlie Brown, he had often felt shy and withdrawn. He was quoted as saying, "There's a melancholy feeling in a lot of cartoonists, because cartooning, like all other humor, comes from bad things happening."

As I stood there, frozen, Colleen managed to come up with a clever line.

"Hi, Mr. Schulz! Do you play a lot of golf?"

He looked a bit dazzled by Colleen, and it took him a few seconds to answer.

"Yes, but I like ice hockey more. I'm doing this tournament because Children's Hospital saved a friend's daughter's life."

His voice was so soft I could barely hear it. Including both of us in an admiring gaze, he spoke up louder. "Hey, I like your sunglasses!"

Colleen's were mirrored, the kind you see yourself reflected in, with fuchsia frames. My frames had side pieces extending from the bottom of the lenses to my ears—a topsy-turvy effect which I'm sure made me look a trifle goofy.

What a friendly man, I thought, *with that sweet smile.*

Just then there was an announcement that dinner was being served, and the golfers began to file out of the room.

"It was nice meeting you ladies," he said.

Our job was finished, so I made a parting remark to Schulz for both of us.

"Goodbye, and I hope you get an eagle-in-one!"

__Dale Robertson__ (1923-2013) made his name in TV Westerns in the 1950's and '60s. He was born in Harrah, Oklahoma. After serving in a tank crew and the combat engineers in North Africa and Europe during World War II, twice-wounded Robertson started his acting career while still on active duty in the

Army. Stationed at San Luis Obispo, California, he had a photograph taken for his mother. A copy of the photo displayed in the photo shop window attracted movie scouts, and the six foot tall, 180-lb. Robertson soon was on his way to Hollywood.

Will Rogers Jr. told him to avoid formal training and keep his own persona. Robertson took his advice. Robertson headlined the TV series Tales of Wells Fargo and Iron Horse. He also served as one of the hosts, along with Ronald Reagan, of the syndicated series Death Valley Days. He was a recipient of the Golden Boot Award in 1985, and was inducted into the Hall of Great Western Performers and the Cowboy Hall of Fame in Oklahoma City. He retired on a ranch near Oklahoma City not far from his birthplace of Harrah.

Charles Schulz *(1922–2000) was a cartoonist best known for the comic strip Peanuts, which featured the characters Charlie Brown and Snoopy, among others. He is regarded as one of the most influential cartoonists of all time, cited as a major influence by many later cartoonists. Peanuts made its first appearance on October 2, 1950, eventually becoming one of the most popular comic strips of all time, as well as one of the most influential. At its height, Peanuts was published daily in 2,600 papers in 75 countries in 21 languages.*

Over the nearly 50 years that Peanuts was published, Schulz drew nearly 18,000 strips. The strips, plus *merchandise and product endorsements, produced revenues of more than $1 billion per year, with Schulz earning an estimated $30 million to $40 million annually. During the life of the strip, Schulz took only one vacation, a five-week break in late 1997 to celebrate his 75th birthday. Awards Schulz received were the National Cartoonists Society's Humor Comic Strip Award in 1962 for Peanuts, and the Society's Elzie Segar Award in 1980. He was the first two-time winner of the Reuben Award for 1955 and 1964, plus the Milton Caniff Lifetime Achievement Award in 1999.*

He was an avid hockey fan. In 1981, Schulz was awarded the Lester Patrick Trophy for outstanding contributions to the sport of hockey in the U.S., and was inducted into the U.S. Hockey Hall of Fame in 1993. On June 28, 1996, Schulz was honored with a star on the Hollywood Walk of Fame, adjacent to Walt Disney's. In 2002, the Charles Schulz Memorial Museum and Research Center, opened in his hometown of Santa Rosa, where the Sonoma County Airport is named in his honor.

Chapter 14

The FBI and I
Huey Newton

The '50s decade when Dior created the New Look, the New York Giants became the San Francisco Giants, and the Kingston Trio was formed, was one of unbelievable change for me. It was also the decade in which I graduated from college, moved to California, started my teaching career, and got married.

Those three events all impinged on my life in some way. My going-away outfit when I married was inspired by Dior—a navy-blue dress with a pinched-in waist and long full skirt. Ed was excited when the Giants started playing in San Francisco, and not long after we were married we went to hear the Kingston Trio at the Hungry I, a nightclub in the North Beach district of San Francisco. The place started the careers of Barbra Streisand, Mort Sahl, Bill

Cosby, Glenn Yarborough, the Kingston Trio, and a host of others.

An influence on culture as well as literature in the '50's was the Beat Generation; however, everything to do with the Beats was out of my realm. Ed and I were the epitome of conformism with a house (bought for $20,000), a beagle puppy, and hopes for starting a family. We held down jobs which afforded us a certain amount of self-respect, just like our parents had done, and although we drank moderately, we never thought about doing drugs. We went to church, looked down on anyone who chose not to work, and if asked, would have said that we didn't consider capitalism at all evil. That would have meant that Ed's illustration work, done in the service of capitalistic advertising, was evil also.

Ed earned $325 a month, and was overjoyed to have a wage-earning spouse. We were both wet behind the ears, and eager to get on with our lives together.

Racial unrest was growing, and black movements were rising up in protest. In 1956, whites bombed four African-American churches and the homes of Martin Luther King and Ralph Abernathy. In 1957, the governor of Arkansas obstructed the integration of Little Rock High School, using the National Guard to block nine students. President Eisenhower intervened, using federal troops to integrate the school.

Martin Luther King and his wife visited India in 1959, where King discussed the philosophy of nonviolence with Mahatma Gandhi's followers. In the wake of the assassination of Malcolm X and the shooting by police in San Francisco of an unarmed black teen in 1961, Huey Newton and Bobby Seale founded the Black Panthers in the Bay Area. The history of the Black Panthers is well documented on the Internet. Let me state briefly that, in my opinion, it was a violent movement founded for virtuous reasons, and later weakened and undermined by the FBI.

My first teaching job was at Woodrow Wilson Junior High, in a neighborhood of Oakland known as the Temescal district. Many families were of Italian descent, and a third or so were African-American. The children were from families who kept them clean, well-clothed, and mostly well-behaved.

Of course there were a few troublemakers, and I always seemed to get a bunch of them in my classes. No doubt some of my students acted out because, even though I tried to speak authoritatively and present a dignified front, I was very young and hadn't the foggiest idea of how to maintain discipline. Only ten years older than the kids, fresh out of college with no prior teaching experience, I had struggled to find a job teaching art. I was finally hired because I promised to obtain a degree in Special Education.

I was issued a temporary credential, and over the next year and a half attended San Francisco State to get the needed units. At Woodrow, I taught two periods of art to normal kids, and three periods of what we then called the Mentally Retarded, children now less offensively labeled 'Learning Disabled.' These slow-learning kids were stuck with inexperienced me trying to teach them math, English, and Social Studies.

Each morning, the school had a 15-minute Homeroom, where we gathered a group of thirty or so students for announcements and attendance keeping. (The Special Ed kids were not included) We teachers had to be scrupulous in keeping track of attendance, and everyone had to sit in his or her assigned seat while we called roll and read off announcements for the day: schedule changes, special assemblies, etc.

I taught at Woodrow for three years. Teaching is always hard work, especially when you are working in a racially diverse, low-income school like Woodrow. But I remember having a lot of laughs there. My faculty friends became pals, and I formed close ties with several: Olga Bier, Gloria Sibilia, and Norma Gandolfo. Olga and Gloria taught art too, and took great pains to help me learn how. Muriel Arends, a tough red-haired gal with a brisk demeanor and heart of gold, later became vice-principal of McClymond's High School in Oakland—that's how tough she was.

I started my job as Miss Hoig. but became Mrs. Diffenderfer when I married. Our principal, Bob Adams, loved to tell a story about me. Since I couldn't maintain order in the three hours I had my Special Ed kids, I used to put inattentive students outside the door of the classroom and have them stand there for five minutes, sometimes longer.

One day I put Geraldine outside the door, a pretty African-American girl who talked non-stop and was a hell-raiser. (She wasn't retarded, only a problem kid and non-learner.) Just my luck, Mr. Adams happened to be passing my classroom that morning. He stopped abruptly and asked, "What are you doing out here, Geraldine? Misbehavior?"

"No sir, Miz *Diffenderfer,*" she replied.

It was eight or ten years after teaching at Woodrow that I got a phone call from the FBI. I had just washed my hair and was standing in my pajamas, a wet towel wrapped around my head. After some polite introductory words, the agent said he wanted to ask my impressions of Huey Newton.

"Who?" I asked.

By then the Black Panthers were notorious, a gun-toting group of radical young black men based in Oakland. There were national headlines and local news stories about the movement and its leaders: Huey Newton, Bobby Seale, Eldridge Cleaver, and Afro-coifed Angela Davis.

"I have absolutely no impressions of Huey Newton! I don't know him and have never met him."

"Ma'am, your name is next to his for three years. This was at Woodrow Wilson Junior High School in Oakland, 48th and Telegraph."

"It *is?*"

"Yes. So, what was he like?"

"I still don't—"

And then I remembered.

Ever-so-slowly, an image of the boy took shape in my head. A thirteen-year-old, light-colored black kid in a worn flannel shirt, slouching in and out of homeroom every morning without uttering a word. Could that be the Huey they wanted me to comment on?

"He might have been in my homeroom, but it only lasted for a quarter of an hour each day. I don't think I ever had him in class, although maybe I did, in one of my art classes. I honestly don't remember. Why are you asking?"

"We're looking into the backgrounds of these Oakland revolutionaries," said the G-man. "We want to know about the influences on their lives."

"Well, *I* wasn't one of his influences," I huffed. "You can take me off your list of subversive teachers right now!"

"We aren't insinuating anything like that. We're just trying to get an idea of the influ—uh—environmental factors affecting these young black men in those years."

"In those years I was a woman nearly overwhelmed by her job. I barely had the energy to prepare lesson plans and turn in grades, let alone take time to lead my students into a life of crime—or treason—or whatever you call what the Black Panthers are doing."

It was eight-thirty in the morning, and my vocabulary was being over-challenged.

"Fine, ma'am. We'll be getting in touch with some of your associates, so you might want to let them know."

"I've lost touch with everyone but Olga Bier. Have you called her?"

"Bier? No, I don't believe so. Oh, wait! Is she the one who runs a musical theater group? She asked me if I could sing or dance. *That* Olga Bier?"

"Yeah, that's Olga. Goodbye. It's been nice talking to you."

That evening when I told Ed about the phone call, he said, "I knew as soon as I met you that you were some kind of subversive pinko."

I threw a rolled-up copy of Pravda at his head.

Huey Newton *(1942–1989) was an African-American political activist and revolutionary who, with Bobby Seale in 1966, co-founded the Black Panther Party. His life was a powerful amalgam of violence and scholarship. The youngest of seven children of a Louisiana sharecropper and Baptist preacher, he was arrested several times as a teenager for criminal offenses, including gun possession and vandalism. He grew up in Oakland, and in his autobiography,* Revolutionary Suicide, *wrote that he grew up ashamed of being black.*

He also wrote:

"During those long years in Oakland public schools, I did not have one teacher who taught me anything relevant to my own life or experience. Not one instructor ever awoke in me a desire to learn more or to question or to explore the worlds of literature, science, and history. All they did was try to rob me of the sense of my own uniqueness and worth, and in the process nearly killed my urge to inquire."

He attended Merritt College in Oakland and the University of Santa Cruz, where he earned a bachelor's degree and later, in 1980, a PhD. At Merritt College he became involved in politics, getting the first African-American history course adopted as part of the college curriculum. He read the works of Karl Marx, Lenin, Malcolm X, Mao Zedong, and Che Guevara. In 1966 he and Seale, influenced by Malcom X, formed the Black Panther Party for Self Defense. The Party sponsored important social programs in Oakland and achieved national and international renown, with prominent liberals sponsoring the movement. However, the Party's violence and gun-bearing activities lost them support in both white and black communities.

In 1964 Newton was accused of stabbing Odell Lee, serving six months in prison. When he got out, there was a shootout with the Oakland Police, a man was killed; Newton was convicted of voluntary manslaughter and sentenced to prison. The state Appellate Court reversed the conviction in 1970 and ordered a new trial, but after two subsequent trials ended in hung juries, the Alameda County Superior Court dismissed charges.

In 1970, after his release from prison, Newton received an invitation to visit the People's Republic of China. He went there in 1971 with comrades Elaine Brown and Robert Bay, and they were greeted in every airport by thousands of people waving copies of the "Little Red Book" and displaying signs that said, "We support the Black Panther Party, down with U.S. imperialism". He wanted to meet Mao Zedong, but instead had two meetings with the first Premier of the People's Republic of China, Zhou Enlai. Newton also had connections with Jim Jones, leader of the Peoples Temple. Jones visited Newton in Havana, Cuba, when he lived there with his wife Gwen Fontaine, and later Newton spoke to Jones's followers by telephone in Jonestown. Newton's cousin, Stanley Clayton, was one of the few residents to escape the area before the 1978 mass suicide of Jones' followers.

There were many more serious incidents of violence in Newton's life. On August 22, 1989, Huey Newton was murdered during a drug buy in West Oakland. His body was cremated and his ashes interred in that city. He was 47 years old.

Chapter 15

A Thousand Times More Magnificent Than Anything : Henry Koerner

I heard that Henry Koerner, a renowned artist from the east, would be teaching an advanced painting summer course at CCAC, where I had taken classes to get my teaching credential. I knew my artistic skills needed sharpening, so I signed up. Koerner had done a great many *Time* covers, which I greatly admired, but I didn't know anything else about him. The covers were different from any others in those days— colorful, painterly portraits of famous people: JFK, John Cheever, Paul Getty, and Barbra Streisand were a few. My favorite was of Maria Callas, which was done in rich tones of reds and browns. It was reported that Koerner insisted on personal sittings for these paintings, and I thought the results were well worth it.

You can view him nowadays on YouTube, sharing his thoughts about painting. One of his quotes is:

> *When I paint a person, it doesn't look like a photo, but it has much more meaning than a camera. I said to Time when they asked if I wanted photographs, I said no, a camera is useless, pictures are one-dimensional, you can't see around them! I will do covers if the people pose for me. It wasn't a commercial job to me, it was to paint the greatest paintings of the 20th century. The work is the greatest thing, execution is the greatest reward. Something gigantic, magnificent. I dream—and my dream is a thousand times more magnificent than anything!*

There were prerequisites for taking his class; we had to have a background in drawing and painting. I was accepted, and on a warm day in June, twelve of us gathered in one of the large studios at CCAC.

Koerner looked to be in his early forties. He was short, stocky, had greying hair and a heavy accent. He was pleasant and engaging, of Austrian descent, yet the farthest thing from a Teutonic personality. However, we knew we were to follow his every stricture; the atmosphere was serious and business-like. The only time I saw him lighten up was when one of our teenage male models showed up wearing a zoot suit, which the boy said had belonged to his older brother.

"Okay!" Koerner said, laughing, "This is new to me, but fine! Let's do it!"

I still have the sketches I did of the model in his bright yellow fedora, yellow coat with padded shoulders, balloon-like maroon pants with reet-pleats, and a watch chain dangling from his belt to his knees.

On the first day, Koerner gave us a list of supplies: drawing pads, oil paints, tool kit, collapsible chair for outdoor sketching, and an ink pen. It was very expensive, but I used it for years. He asked if we knew anyone who might want to pose, and I suggested one of my students, a lovely teenager from Woodrow, Nellie Richardson. She was African-American, very intelligent, and I thought she would be an excellent model. I knew she was from a large family and could use the money. Koerner said fine, so I got her phone number from school, called, and she said she'd like to do it. As for transportation, she said she knew all about city buses.

We alternated outdoor sketching, drawing models in nature, with drawing in class. After Koerner approved one of our sketches, we were assigned to do a painting from that. By the time we were midway through the semester, I'd started my painting of Nellie. I asked her to wear a red blouse, since I wanted to use the colors Koerner had used in the Callas portrait. I copied his style, using subtle shades of green and violet for shadows in the face and clothing. I kept the background simple, broken into large color areas. It turned into the best portrait I'd ever done, and I had it framed and hung it on the wall of our living room.

After Nellie's last day of modeling, I drove her home. When she jumped out of the car, three of her sisters were skipping rope in the front yard, and we all exchanged waves as I drove away.

Seven or eight years passed, and one summer my widowed mother came out to California to keep me and the kids company while Ed went to the Bohemian Grove, a summer encampment of the Bohemian Club, which I thought of as a grown-up Boy Scout camp, with drinking.

Ed and I had been invited to Nellie's wedding, so I took Mom instead. It was held in a historic Victorian house at Defremery Park near downtown Oakland. Nellie looked gorgeous in her wedding dress, and it was a beautiful ceremony, with handsome groom attendants and bevies of excited bridesmaids, mostly Nellie's sisters. Mom and I were escorted down the aisle by tall young men of both races. I assumed they were the groom's pals; Joe Gardere attended St. Mary's College on a basketball scholarship.

It was a kick to see my little mother precede me down the aisle hanging on the arm of one of those giant athletes. As we took our seats, Mom whispered, "If only Gladys could see me now!"

My Aunt Gladys, plump, spoiled, and loud, was one of the most racially-biased people I've ever known. Once, standing in line in Dallas at a fast food place, she must have said something rude, because an even larger black woman turned around and threw a milkshake in her face!

Driving home from the wedding, I said, "I haven't bought Nellie's wedding gift. I don't know what to buy her."

Mom said, "Why don't you give her the portrait you did?"

"Oh no! It's the best I've ever done. I think I'll get her some monogrammed towels."

It was probably two years later when Nellie and I met for lunch. We brought along my two kids and her baby boy, and after we ate, I said, "I have something to give you."

She followed me to my car, and I presented her with the painting. Her face lit up, and she tried to speak, but couldn't. She bumped her baby further up on her hip, took the portrait, and finally said, "Thank you so much, Mrs. Diff! *Thank you!*"

Nellie finished school at Cal State Hayward, near Oakland, and became a teacher, then later became an elementary school principal in that city. She had a distinguished career, and Ed and I were very honored to attend her retirement dinner many years later.

> **Henry Koerner** *(1915-1991) an Austrian-born American painter and graphic designer, was best known for his Magical Realist works of the 1940's and portrait covers for Time magazine. Born in Vienna to Jewish parents, Koerner was trained in graphic design. Following Hitler's annexation of Austria he fled to the United States, settling in New York. As a commercial artist in Manhattan, he achieved success and many awards.*
>
> *In 1943, the Office of War Information hired Koerner, where he worked with artist Ben Shahn. Shahn's pictorial style, along with the photography of Walker*

Evans and German Neue Sachlichkeit painters, inspired Koerner's painting. In the U.S. Army, he made war posters and documented everyday life. Later Koerner worked at sketching defendants at the Nuremberg trials. Discharged in 1946, Koerner returned to Vienna to discover that his parents and brother had been deported and killed.

In Berlin he painted his first major works; these were exhibited to international acclaim. Returning to New York, he exhibited his Berlin works in an exhibition at Midtown Galleries. Life magazine wrote of the show, "No new artist in years has been accorded the sudden unanimous praise received by Koerner." From 1952 to 1953, Koerner was Artist-in-Residence at Pennsylvania College for Women (now Chatham University) in Pittsburg, PA, where he met his second wife, Joan Marlene Frasher. From 1955 to 1967 he painted over fifty portrait covers for Time. Koerner died in 1991 in Austria following complications from a hit-and-run accident on his bicycle. He is buried in Pittsburgh's Frick Cemetery. His son Joseph Koerner is an art historian and film-maker.

Chapter 16

Blundering Among the Bierstadts
Paul Mills & Steven Zellerbach

Our little family was growing. The children loved Punkin and Shammy, and Ed was thriving in the illustration world, serving one year as president of the San Francisco Illustrator's Club.

Our little daughter had shown an early love for music, so we started her on piano lessons. I took her for weekly lessons for twelve years, and from the time she was eight and all through her teens, she took part in recitals. Learning to play Gershwin's "Rhapsody in Blue" was only one of her musical achievements.

An only child, Ed was slowly evolving into a loving and caring parent. He played catch with our son and shared piano duets with our daughter.

The kids liked school. They went to elementary school in Montclair, where Craig was a second-grader, and one night when I was helping him into his pajamas, he said, "Guess what, Mommy! I got to draw and color all day!"

"What?" I said. "How come?"

"The teacher said, if I didn't wanta work, I could draw and color until my arms and neck and shoulders ached!"

This sounded all wrong, but it wasn't until I told the story to my horrified mother-in-law that I decided I should go for a conference with the principal. I knew that Craig's teacher was a middle-aged woman, but I couldn't believe she was sadistic.

Sitting in the principal's office, I learned that one day instead of doing the assigned lesson, Craig had drawn pictures all around the edges of the paper. But his parents were both artists, so what would be so unusual about that? Also, the old biddy told the principal that on the playground, he burst into tears when one of the other boys stepped on a spider.

Evidently the teacher had been disgusted by our little boy's behavior.

"*Uh-oh—better go easy on the Albert Schweitzer talks,*" I thought. I had once talked to him about Dr. Schweitzer's theory of the sanctity of all life, and read aloud the physician's words, "We must fight against the spirit of unconscious cruelty with which we treat animals. Animals suffer as much as we do."

Now I was seething with anger. "I don't think our son should be made to feel like an outcast just because he's artistic and sensitive!"

Mrs. Palumbo tried to soothe my feelings. "I think we'll test your son. He probably has a high I. Q."

She went on to say something about my possible brilliance as well, and by the time I left her office, I'd forgotten what I came in for.

It was becoming clear to me that I was never going to be a famous artist. I was in my thirties, soon to be forty, and there was no sign of it. I was happy about Ed's success as an illustrator, but that was him.

I'd been doing quick portraits of the students at school carnivals. I was happy to do my bit, and decided that I should try to generate some income for my own family. I put an ad in the local paper and slowly—very slowly—began to acquire clients for both pastel and acrylic portraits. I had stopped using oils because of the odor; acrylics were easier to deal with. The paint quality is almost identical, but you can still find artists who will argue about oil vs. acrylic until their faces turn cerulean blue.

I was helped by my husband's critical eye, as well as by his Nikon camera, which I used to photograph my subjects. Another aid to my portraiture was his *camera lucia*, housed in his large basement studio. A camera lucia, which Ed and his illustrator friends called a 'lucy', is a device which reflects photographs onto canvas or paper, enabling the artist to faithfully reproduce the features of the subject.

It was used before the time of Vermeer, and is shown being used by him in the movie *Girl with a Pearl Earring*.

Besides individual portraits, I did many groups of siblings, often with the family dog and cat thrown in for no extra charge.

I worked in the breakfast area connected to our kitchen. The light was good, and paint and chalk dust couldn't damage the tile floor. This was my studio for thirty-seven years.

By the time I stopped doing portraits sometime in the 2000s, I had gone up in price from $50 to $500 per child. My portraits are in many East Bay homes. I never made a lot of money, but it was an outlet for my creative juices, and I think the families enjoyed the paintings. Moreover, I got a kick out of doing it! I've always liked children, and I found that dealing with the mothers was almost always an enjoyable experience.

Sadly, there were a few women who found ways to throw a monkey wrench into my small operation. There was the mother who let me take three rolls of film of her little cherub, then decided not to go through with the project. Another mom told me to change her teenage daughter's lips from thin to full. Instead, I painted a true likeness, and Mom paid me, but I heard that she never hung the portrait and always kept it in a closet. I always felt sad about that one, a group of three enchanting blond sisters. I wasn't repentant, just sad.

Then there was the mom who called me five years after I had done her two kids, wanting to know if I could insert a newly-acquired little brother between the first two. I said no, it would ruin the composition, and thus the integrity of the picture. She was very insistent, so I eventually hung up on her.

One day a mother brought ten outfits for her eight-year-old son, and wanted me to photograph him in all of them so we could choose the most flattering. We were able to compromise on three.

I did hundreds of portraits over a career of many years. My career never spread far; I was a small fish in a small pond, enjoying the swim.

I couldn't have made it through those years without some kind of intellectual stimulation, so when I heard that the projected Oakland Museum was looking for docents and that my friend Georgia Radford was going to sign up, I said *me too!* The museum was to be three museums in one: Art, Natural Sciences and History.

Georgia and I hoped to be art docents.

We started classes in a room in the Oakland Auditorium, and those three years of study were much more intense than my art history studies in college.

Paul Mills, the sparkplug of the museum and our first instructor, was handsome and soft-spoken; a man almost alone when he first tried to bring California art to the forefront of Bay Area culture. A graduate student in art history at UC Berkeley, Paul proposed putting together a collection celebrating the art of California, and a new building to house it. No one was interested, but he and other museum supporters went ahead. They were able to buy works cheaply, acquiring paintings by noted landscape artists such as William Keith, Thomas Hill, and the group called "The Society of Six."

In 1957 Mills put together an exhibition featuring the work of painters who would gain fame as leaders of the Bay Area Figurative movement: David Park, Elmer Bischoff, and Richard Diebenkorn among them. Paul's University of California master's thesis on Park was later published as a book, *The New Figurative Art of David Park*.

I began to make friends with the other docents. Georgia was a graduate of Vassar, and I liked her ironic sense of humor. When we weren't attending lectures, watching films, or taking notes, we liked to chat and giggle together. She and her architect husband Warren lived in Berkeley in a home Warren designed. Later, Georgia and Warren Radford co-authored *Outdoor Sculpture in San Francisco* and *Sculpture in the Sun*.

Another Berkeley docent had an elegant home near the UC campus, and she invited us over to see her Diebenkorn paintings. Most impressive!

Ada Wong, married to architect Worley Wong, was chirpy and cheerful. Ada continued to work at the museum for many years, serving on the Women's Board and participating in fundraising activities like the White Elephant Sale. Her husband Worley happened to be the architect for our small contemporary home in Montclair.

Not all the docents were the height of culture and breeding. One had a bad case of B.O, and once boasted of traveling for three weeks in Europe with only one small carry-on bag.

"*Uh-huh*," I thought.

We took classes for three years, covering almost every art period, because the building didn't get finished on time. We started with the Greeks and Romans and ended with Abstract Expressionism. In between were the Middle Ages, Early and High Renaissance; and Northern Renaissance.

We studied the European eras, with an emphasis on Impressionism and Post-Impressionism. Our teachers, mostly from the University of California and San Francisco State, also lectured on Asian art, and Paul insisted that we spend two months on California painting. Therese Heyman and Hazel Bray lectured on photography and crafts; and their knowledge was breathtaking.

When the museum was finished in September 1969, we docents began acting as guides. If the number of schoolchildren who have gone through the Oakland Museum were totaled, and no doubt it has been—it must be a staggering count.

Once Paul Mills asked if I would do a special assignment. I'm sure his request had something to do with raising money.

He asked me to conduct businessman Steven Zellerbach on a private tour. Zellerbach was chairman of the board of Crown Zellerbach Corporation, one of the largest paper companies in the world. Mr. Zellerbach contributed hundreds of thousands of dollars to the arts, and one of his biggest contributions was to UC Berkeley for a performing arts theater. Zellerbach Hall on the UC campus has hosted thousands of programs through the years. I once saw the Bolshoi Ballet perform there.

As for Paul's request, I said I would be honored, and a few days later, met Mr. Zellerbach and Paul at the entrance to the museum. Paul introduced us, then said he was leaving the visitor in my care, and walked away.

I guessed Mr. Z. to be in his mid-'70s. He reminded me of my old friend J. C. Penney, but unlike Penney, he had a jovial exterior, and I knew right away that we were going to get along.

I began with early California landscape paintings, including our collection of Gold Rush artwork. I tried to stay chatty but brief, and he didn't ask many questions. Twenty minutes later, when we came to the huge and magnificent Yosemite landscape paintings of Alfred Bierstadt, William Keith, and Thomas Hill, he reacted the same way everyone did.

"Beautiful!" he breathed.

"Now," I said, "I want to show you my favorite part of the museum, the Arthur and Lucia Mathews collection."

The Mathews were a creative Oakland couple who personified the American Craftsman school. The museum owned countless examples of their furniture, lamps, vases, ceramics, and paintings. For more than two decades in the first part of the 20th century, Arthur and Lucia Matthews were the most influential artists in the Northern California art scene.

"And here's my favorite painting, Lucia Mathews' "Oranges, Portrait of a Red Haired Girl." It was done in 1910. Mr. Zellerbach, she studied with *Whistler!*"

"Why is this your favorite?" he asked. "Is it because it's by a woman?"

"Good question. No, it's because it's so fresh! Notice how the child's head and shoulders are treated with minimal detail, while the fruit and leaves backing her figure are handled more realistically. But not so realistically that they detract from the treatment of the figure."

I took a breath. "I know you responded to the big landscape paintings the same way the public does, but I wanted to show you that our museum contains many subtle and sensitive works as well."

I stood there, almost out of breath. It must have been obvious that this wasn't part of my usual patter.

He looked at me, then at the picture, then at me again. "I believe you have convinced me."

I began to walk him through the "Society of Six" collection. He was familiar with the group, and when he made an admiring comment about Logan's watercolors, I mentioned that my husband had once worked for him as an illustrator.

Lastly we came to the modern California painters: Diebenkorn, Park, Ramos, and Thiebaud. He seemed familiar with these artists, too, mentioning that he'd met Wayne Thiebaud at UC Davis.

We parted a few minutes later. He thanked me for my help, and I said it had been a pleasure. Then he headed off to touch base once more with Paul.

I didn't know what kind of impression I'd made. Did I hurt or help the museum? More specifically, did I raise any money? I wondered if it had been wrong to go on and on about one specific painting. And had I sounded negative about the Bierstadts and Hills?

Days later I ran into Paul and, fishing for a compliment, said I hoped Mr. Zellerbach had enjoyed the tour I gave him.

"Oh yes, thanks for your extra time! Mr. Z. said you were something of a firebrand!"

Was that a good thing or bad?

Paul was smiling, so I couldn't really tell, and I guess I'll never know.

***Paul Mills** (1931-2004) former director of the Oakland Museum of California made California art the museum's focus and organized the first show of Bay Area Figurative painting. In 1953, Mills became part-time curator at the old Oakland Museum of Art. The next year he proposed putting together a collection and a new building to house it. It would celebrate the art of California, a subject of little interest to the art world then. Mills and supporters were able to buy works cheaply from Stanford University and other institutions, and also acquired paintings by noted landscape artists such as William Keith, Thomas Hill and the Bay Area group called The Society of Six.*

Mills brought a scholarly background combined with a down-to-earth manner that made him suited for the task of creating a museum of California. With a hard-working band of docents, he laid a historical foundation for the collection, combing through old newspapers and searching out descendants of artists. The movie Beginners, with Christopher Plummer as Paul Mills and Ewan McGregor as his son Mike, is based on a book Mike wrote about his father.

Stephen Zellerbach *(1927-2011) philanthropist, businessman, community activist and 4th generation San Franciscan, will be remembered for a lifelong commitment to the Bay Area. After serving in World War II in the Navy, Mr. Zellerbach came home to the Bay Area and completed a business degree at U.C. Berkeley. He began his business career at the Zellerbach Paper Company, which was founded in San Francisco in 1870 by his great-grandfather, Anthony Zellerbach.*

He co-founded a car rental business and McCutchan Publishing Corporation, next venturing into the wine business and launching Stephen Zellerbach Vineyards with his wife, Cecile "CiCi" Zellerbach. Among other credits, he was former president of the San Francisco Ballet Association, sat on the Landmarks Board of the SF Opera and the board of the SF Bay Area Red Cross, and for over 44 years was Chairman of the Commission for the Preservation of Pioneer Jewish Cemeteries and Landmarks. A lifetime member of the St. Francis Yacht Club, he loved boating and sailing *on the Bay. Mr. Zellerbach created many innovative sculptures which adorned his Healdsburg property. After a $1 million gift was given toward completion of the facility, Zellerbach Hall on the U.C. Berkeley campus was named in honor of Isadore and Jennie Zellerbach and dedicated in 1968.*

Chapter 17

Hindsight
George Shearing

One rainy weekend we were invited to a party by a musician friend of my husband's, Ed MacKay. Ed was married to a wealthy socialite, Cynthia, and they lived in a great old Victorian house, one of the famous Painted Ladies at Steiner and Hayes in San Francisco. In those days the houses were not nearly as celebrated and photographed as they are now.

About 48,000 houses in the Victorian and Edwardian styles were built in San Francisco between 1849 and 1915, and many were painted in bright colors. One of the best-known groups of "Painted Ladies" is the row of Victorian houses at 710–720 Steiner Street, across from Alamo Square park. It is sometimes known as "Postcard Row." They are also known as the Seven Sisters, one of which we spent the evening in on that memorable night. This block appears frequently in media and mass-market photographs of the city, and has appeared in an estimated 70 movies.

Cynthia had come over from England during World War II when her parents sent her to San Francisco just before the Blitz, and Ed MacKay married her after she divorced her first husband, a descendant of one of the 'Big Four' families of San Francisco.

The house was decorated in the English style, antiques and chintz.

My only faux pas of the evening (that I know of) was when I said to our host, "You have some fantastic antiques, and we're shopping for some, too! Where'd you get them?"

"They were in the family," he said. "What would you like to drink?"

Egg on my face—again.

Brought up short by Ed Mackay's offhand reply, I realized I must have sounded like some vulgar parvenu, and all my old feelings of rustic inferiority came rushing back. I shook them off; after all, I had been invited here tonight, so I must have passed muster somewhere along the way.

For quite a few years, my Ed and I had been shopping for used furniture and antiques, mostly around Oakland, Berkeley, and Vallejo. Antiques were cheaper than the new stuff, and besides, they added a touch of whimsicality to our décor. We often shopped in Gold Country stores, always returning home with an old clock or chest, once with two old wooden balustrades from a staircase. These made big attractive candle-holders for either side of our fireplace in Lafayette.

Ed's parents owned a few authentic pieces. One was a Chippendale chair which came from an eastern branch of Mig's family, and we inherited it after Mig died and George broke up housekeeping. They had some silver too, and old family drawings and silhouette portraits, all handed down through the generations.

Once, after dropping Ed off at the bus station on San Pablo Avenue in a derelict part of Oakland, I forced my way into a second-hand shop, complete with dirty windows and hordes of battered rickety tables and cabinets. The young storekeeper opened the shop to me at 6:30 in the morning, and you could hardly move around, it was so crowded. I discovered a small chopping block with chunky legs, and bought it for a scandalously low price. Somehow the man squeezed it into my car.

When we arrived at the Mackays, we found that it wasn't a large party but a small dinner, and the guest of honor was the famous blind pianist, George Shearing, Shearing was a member of the Bohemian Club and often performed at Grove encampments.

Ed had done his portrait a few months before.

The men had a jam session before dinner with Ed MacKay on bass, Ed on trombone, Ken McCaulou on alto sax, and Shearing playing his unique style of piano.

We ladies sat nearby, enjoying the music and getting to know one another. I already knew Cynthia MacKay and

Gail, Ken's wife, but had never met Ellie Shearing. Ellie was a singer, had a big smile and hearty laugh, and I warmed to her right away. Our hostess was an attractive brunette with all the posh and polish you'd expect of English gentry (I think her father was a Lord). Gail, like me, was a suburban housewife and mother. She was petite and very pretty.

When we finally sat down to dinner, I sat on George's right.

A brilliant raconteur, sitting with his head tilted and eyes closed, he rattled off one joke after another, and when I laughed loudly at one of them, he suddenly turned and ran his hand over my face.

I jumped, startled.

Ellie said, "He wants to see your laugh."

"Oh," I said.

"What does she look like?" George asked.

"Like Valerie Perrine," said Ellie. Perrine was a young actress of the seventies who played Lenny Bruce's wife in *Lenny*. I didn't think I looked anything like her, but was flattered anyway.

The copious amount of wine poured by two serving women caused the men to turn red in the face—except for George, who stayed very pale—and the women to get rather giggly.

Suddenly, conversation swung to politics and to Gerald Ford's pardon of Nixon.

A month after Nixon announced his resignation, Ford issued the former president a "full, free and absolute" pardon for any crimes he committed while in office. Almost everyone at the table agreed it was the best thing for the country, but opinions varied as to whether Tricky Dick should have been pardoned at all.

Ed and I stood at the door with the host and hostess when George and Ellie left. George put his arm through hers and, as she led him out, he tilted his head and chirped a very British, "Cheerio, all!"

> *George Shearing (1919- 2011) was the youngest of nine children. Shearing was born in London into a working-class family. His father delivered coal and his mother cleaned trains by night. Blind from birth, George showed musical aptitude, memorizing tunes he heard on the radio and picking them out on the family piano. He took lessons and continued his studies at the Linden Lodge school for blind children. Offered university musical scholarships, he turned them down in favor of work as a solo pianist in local pubs, achieving prominence with an all-blind stage orchestra in 1937. Heavily influenced by Teddy Wilson and Fats Waller, he played alongside visiting American stars like tenor-saxophonist Coleman Hawkins. He played in bands fronted by prominent leaders, including the French jazz violinist Stéphane Grappelli, with whom he recorded.*
>
> *Shearing's recording of "September in the Rain," 1949, sold 900,000 copies. Shearing's quintet toured in the U.S. endlessly, recorded incessantly and played at the best clubs in America. Credited with some 300 compositions, Shearing gained his greatest success with "Lullaby of Birdland" (1952). He performed for three*

U.S. presidents and for a royal command performance, and was touched when the George Shearing Centre, providing facilities for disabled people in Battersea, was named in his honor. A naturalized American citizen, he never wavered in his affection for Britain, returning in summers to the Cotswold house he had bought with second wife Ellie Geffert, avidly following cricket on BBC Radio's Test Match Special, and indulging his penchant for English humor. Appointed OBE (Order of the British Empire) in 1996, he was knighted in 2007. His autobiography Lullaby of Birdland *appeared in 2004.*

Cynthia Vansittart MacKay *(1922-2023), whose active and varied life linked two nations and two centuries, died on March 23 at her San Francisco home after a brief illness. She was 100 years old.*

Mrs. MacKay was born in London in 1922. Her father, Sir Robert (later Lord) Vansittart was a diplomat, author, and outspoken opponent of Germany's Nazi regime. He was a friend of Sir Winston Churchill, whom Mrs. MacKay also knew and considered one of her heroes. Mrs. MacKay was in school when war broke out in 1939. As head of the British Foreign Office in the 1930's and still active in intelligence circles, Sir Robert feared for his daughter's safety. So he sent her to live in California with San Francisco Chronicle publisher George Cameron and his wife, who were close family friends.

In 1941 she married railroad heir Frederick Crocker Whitman of San Francisco, then serving in the U.S. Navy. The marriage ended in divorce 14 years later. In 1956 she married Edward H. MacKay Jr., a San Francisco businessman, and the union lasted until his death in 1995.

Mrs. MacKay became a U.S. citizen in 1947. She was an avid reader, especially books of English history. She enjoyed Masterpiece Theatre television, in particular "Upstairs, Downstairs," which she often watched with her daughter. Mrs. MacKay was an admirer of the British Crown, Queen Elizabeth in particular. Like the Queen, she loved dogs, especially Corgis, and the MacKay family once had a Corgi pet.

Mrs. MacKay's 100th birthday was celebrated at a family party. She received congratulatory letters from President Joe Biden and California Governor Gavin Newsom.

She is survived by her daughter, Tania Whitman Stepanian, sons Michael Robert Vansittart Whitman, Jonathan Crocker Whitman, Kevin Crocker Whitman, Robert Vansittart MacKay, Donald James Edward MacKay, stepson Edward (Ned) H. MacKay III, eight grandchildren and two great-grandchildren.

Edward H. MacKay *died October 23, 1995 at his San Francisco home after a long fight with leukemia. He was 86. Born in Clinton, Mass., and educated at*

the Phillip Exeter Academy in New Hampshire and the Massachusetts Institute of Technology, Mr. MacKay spent many years traveling and working in Europe and Asia. In the late 1930's he worked for American Express in Asia, and after serving as assistant manager of its Shanghai office for six months during World War II, he was in a civilian prisoner-of-war camp. Repatriated to the United States in 1942 as part of an exchange brokered by the international Red Cross, he went to work for the Office of War Information in Hawaii. After the war, Mr. MacKay settled in San Francisco and worked for a number of businesses.

An accomplished amateur musician and competitive swimmer, Mr. MacKay was an active member of the Bohemian Club and the Olympic Club. He was a past president of the San Francisco branch of the English Speaking Union, a past trustee of Grace Cathedral and of the Robert Louis Stevenson in Pebble Beach, Monterey County. He is survived by his wife of 40 years, Cynthia Vansittart Mackay; sons Robert and Donald of Petaluma, and Edward of Pleasant Hill; a sister Miriam Horne of Bradford, Mass.; and one granddaughter.

Chapter 18

St. Helena Swells
Lord Alexander Hesketh

By now the reader will have stumbled onto the fact that Ed and I were in over our heads. We always struggled with money, so hanging out with the upper class was a bit of a strain. But it was only one part of our lives. The rest of the time we dealt with making ends meet and weeding our own garden—plus every cliché you've ever heard about keeping up with the Joneses.

Or, in this case, the Vanderbilts.

A few months after our dinner at the Mackays we were invited to an August luncheon in St. Helena, Napa County.

We didn't have a hostess, only a host, a short, balding gentleman, that's all I remember about him. The house was a one-story ranch style, surrounded by one of the most beautiful gardens I'd ever seen, much less been a guest in. Masses of hydrangeas, hostas, roses, and Japanese maples.

The party started off with a bang when Al and De De Wilsey arrived in their helicopter, setting it down on the immense green lawn as the rest of us watched.

Wilsey was one of the Bay Area's most prominent businessmen, a philanthropist who gave millions of dollars to San Francisco's arts institutions and schools. De De's great-grandfather started Dow Chemical, and both had had a few high-flying marriages before the current one.

After Al Wilsey died, De De became an important philanthropist in San Francisco as well, mostly tied to the city's fine art museums.

Ed's jazz group was there for entertainment, of course, with Ed Mackay on bass fiddle. I waved to Cynthia, who was standing on the other side of the crowd.

After a period of cocktails, wine, and socializing, all of us were seated outdoors at a long table. It was covered with a lime-green tablecloth, a half-dozen flower arrangements, and an army of glassware. The sun was shining, the birds were twittering—I felt as if I'd landed in a little piece of heaven.

I'd shopped for something to wear and had finally found it for more money than I wanted to pay, but I loved it—a long-sleeved, collared white eyelet shirt. The eyelet holes were pretty large, and I said to the salesgirl, "Do you think I'm too old for this?"

Of course she said no, adding, "This is a Diane von Furstenberg copy!"

I wore a white bra under the blouse, along with new white pants, and Ed said I looked glamorous. He didn't always comment on what I was wearing, though I remember once he insisted I change out of a chartreuse-and-green striped shift because he said I looked like a walking dill pickle.

Somehow I ended up sitting between my husband and, can you believe it?—an English lord.

Alexander Hesketh was only around twenty-five, but very polished and gallant. He was tall, had an engaging smile, and was wearing a light-blue linen blazer, open-collared white shirt, no tie. He was already a little spiffed, and after he greeted me with a kiss on the cheek, I said, "Isn't this a beautiful garden, Lord Hesketh?"

"Call me Alex. Smashing, but I'd love you to see mine. You have a nice tan. How'd you get it?"

"Tennis."

"Oh, and your Chris Evert just won Wimbledon. Aren't you enormously proud?" He laughed a booming laugh.

"And Jimmy Connors beat Borg in that long, long match at the U. S. Open," I said. "How about *that!*"

He then veered off into a long discussion about cricket, which Ed seemed interested in, but I wasn't.

Soon we began diving into the food, and since we all received printed menus, I can tell you what we had:

Leeks in Vinaigrette | Fig and Goat Cheese Salad
Scallops in white wine | French Plum Tart

The afternoon wore on, with much laughter and joviality around the table. Al Wilsey stood up and told a funny story about sailing in the Black Islands.

Gradually the day cooled, and the birds grew quiet in the trees. Around four, it was time to leave. I was entering the bathroom as Cynthia was coming out, and she didn't return my smile. On the contrary, her face was a study in frostiness.

"No wonder you excite attention, my dear," she said, "dressing like a woman on Capp Street."

I couldn't believe my ears. My mouth dropped open, and I didn't say anything; I was too shocked. Usually I could muster up a response to any sort of remark, but now was struck silent.

I walked away and tried to brush it off. My day wasn't ruined, although I knew this was the end of any friendship between us.

I cried a little in the car going home, but when Ed asked what was wrong, I just said I was tired and had had too much to drink.

Later I thought of several brilliant replies I could have made to Cynthia's spiteful remark.

One was, "You should try it sometime, come walk the streets with me!"

Another was, "I'm sorry I don't dress like you British expatriates, wearing tweed in the middle of August!"

Except she wasn't wearing tweed, but an expensive-looking cotton dress, no doubt from Saks Fifth Avenue.

I'm sure it grated on her that she didn't get to sit next to her countryman. Her father was part of the English aristocracy, and she and the young Britisher would have had a lot to talk about.

I had one of my gratifying dreams that night.

Cynthia, Lord Hesketh, and I were wafting together above a country road, and suddenly a floating herd of cows appeared in front of us. Alex and I soared above and continued on our way, but Cynthia walked directly into the herd and stepped into a big floating cow flop.

> **Lord Alexander Hesketh/3rd Baron Hesketh** *(1950-) As a British Peer, Alexander Hesketh automatically became a member of the House of Lords upon the untimely death of his father, Baron Hesketh at age 39. After college, he went on to work for Dean Witter in San Francisco before returning to England to manage his family's businesses.*
>
> *He took no active part in politics until he met and was encouraged by Prime Minister Margaret Thatcher. He held the office of Parliamentary Under-Secretary of State, Department for Environment and Minister of State in the Department of Trade and Industry until 1999. In 2003, he became treasurer of the Conservative Party, resigning in 2006.*

In 1972 he founded Hesketh Racing, and later was president of the British Racing Drivers' and formed Hesketh Motorcycles. In 1994 Hesketh helped set up British Mediterranean Airways (BMED), becoming chairman until early 2007 when BMED was purchased by UK Airline BMI. He subsequently served as an "independent director" of Air Astana, the national carrier of Kazakhstan.

In 1977, Hesketh was appointed a Knight Commander of the Order of the British Empire (KBE). That same year, Lord Hesketh married Hon. Claire Georgina Watson. Together, they are the parents of three children.

Chapter 19

Thoroughly Modern Mollie
Mollie Poupeney

I subordinated my talent and drive to that of my husband's. Ed was making his living—*our* living—as an illustrator, and I wanted him to succeed for all our sakes. He liked me to take part in his musical and social life, too, and I was more than willing, since it offered the excitement I wasn't finding anywhere else.

But I needed to find an outlet for my creative energy. I'd been doing children's portraits since my own children were small. My efforts brought in relatively little income, but I was satisfying the drive I'd had since I was eight, when, with Daddy's fond approval, I sat in the back of the family drugstore drawing Mickey and Minnie Mouse.

One commission was of a brother and sister, plus the Dalmatian Rowdy and Tigger the cat. These were the Moxley kids, John and Martha, who lived down the street.

Their mom, blond blue-eyed Dorthy *(correct spelling)* had become one of my best friends. Dorthy and I liked to team up shopping for rugs, bedspreads, and blenders—we called it 'terrorizing the merchants'. We became embroiled in numerous funny situations, and we did a lot of laughing. Ed and I liked Dave very much too, and the four of us became friends.

Not only did she commission the portrait, but Dorthy bought several of my paintings. She was one of my early boosters, which I welcomed then and appreciate to this day.

By the seventies, I was beginning to want more of a challenge, something to make my juices flow. My brother and husband were piling up accomplishments; Ed with illustration and my brother Stan Hoig writing Indian and Oklahoma history.

I was becoming more and more intrigued with literature, and in the late sixties, my cousin Fran and I began to venture into San Francisco to take University of California Extension classes. Her children were grown, and she was divorced with time on her hands. Over the span of several years we took courses in modern Russian literature, William Faulkner, and T. S. Eliot.

I became caught up in Faulkner, read practically everything he wrote. I admired the fictional world of

Yoknapatawpha County, because his southerners sounded a lot like the characters in my hometown.

Other literary influences around that time were Virginia Woolf's *A Room of One's Own* and Alice Munro's short stories. After reading *Lives of Girls and Women*, I was Munro's acolyte forever.

I didn't know any women who could be inspirations for the creative life. All my friends were housewives, tennis players, and party-goers. There was my writing friend Colleen Brooks, but she never discussed her writing, and our friendship remained on the surface.

There was something pushing me to become more productive, and I was bursting with original concepts, all of them going nowhere. These ideas couldn't be expressed through art, but perhaps could be brought out in writing. My brain loved to wander among ideas, facts, and memories. Could I tie all those together into a new entity—a unique shape?

I loved reading fiction, so why not try writing it?

Finally, I took the next step. Feeling the urge to tell stories about my hometown, I took a course in fiction writing, another UC Extension class. My cousin had remarried and had no interest in the subject, so I went alone to sign up. The evening class was on the Berkeley campus two nights a week, and that was when I met Mollie Poupeney.

Mollie and I lived in adjoining towns but had never met, even though we were both artists. Mollie fully exemplified the word; she was a renowned potter whose huge coiled pots were shown in art galleries in all of Contra Costa county.

Just now, though, she was focused on writing a coming-of-age story. As I was, without knowing it.

My background was much sunnier than Mollie's. I focused on writing funny stories centered in our little town in the Dust Bowl, many of them set in the family drugstore, but through her writing I learned that Mollie's Oregon family was very poor, with a father who was not only a drunk but an abuser.

I got to know Mollie well, because after every class a group of us met for coffee at a local café. There were no bars in that part of Berkeley; an ordinance prohibited the sale of alcohol within a mile of the campus. We met around a big table, slurped coffee, and discussed a myriad of subjects. Our writing instructor, a middle-aged man whose name I've forgotten, occasionally joined us, and in that setting once gave me some excellent advice.

"You'll never get readers to stay interested in mere anecdotes, you need a plot." That was the impetus for *The Wind Came Running*, which I published years later.

Mollie had a few rough edges. She wore baggy corduroys or jeans and never bothered with makeup. Her best features were her mop of curly grey-brown hair and lively brown eyes. Her speech was direct and insightful, and one evening she happened to mention Betty Friedan.

"Who's Betty Friedan?" I asked.

She stared at me as if I were a two-headed baboon.

"You mean you haven't heard of *The Feminine Mystique?*"

"Well. of course I've *heard* of it! I just didn't know she was the author."

"Have you read it?"

"Uh, no."

I was usually in defensive mode with Mollie, but it wasn't her fault, it was mine.

"Take a look at it, kiddo. It's a whole new way of looking at women. You won't be sorry."

I went out the next day and bought a copy, and didn't put it down until I'd finished it. I had to take time out to cook meals and get the kids off to high school, but I read it in two days. Friedan makes a strong case for broadening women's roles in society, and she makes an equally good case for a woman's need to find fulfilment in a calling, career, or job; something other than housewifery and maternal chores.

When I next saw Mollie, I said I totally agreed with almost everything that Friedan said.

"Whaddya mean, *almost?*" Her mahogany eyes bored into mine.

"Well, *everything*, then! I don't think women can find total fulfilment in marriage and motherhood, and they'll be unhappy if they try. And I know we shouldn't try to live through our children. I guess that's why I'm here, to find personal fulfillment!" I paused, taking a drag on my cigarette. "But I'm here mainly because I want to learn how to tell my story."

She nodded, softening her gaze. "Yeah. Me too."

I began to admire Mollie more and more for her energy and honesty. She was far apart from the women I usually surrounded myself with, and I sensed a depth in her that was lacking in me and my friends.

It's odd, but I don't remember a single other soul from the class, and I remember Mollie a lot better than the instructor.

Here are some things I recall her saying:

"Women don't have to be doormats, they can be flying carpets!" and "My daughter wanted me to stay home to shorten her prom dress, but I said, 'Get your brother to do it, he went to the prom last year!'"

And "Every time Leon asks me to clean out the refrigerator, I tell him to go clean out the garage. Nothing shuts him up faster!"

Of all the remarks I heard her utter, the one I liked best was, "Writing the story of my life is like trying to collect fireflies in a bottle, and the bottle has no bottom and no top."

Besides her magnificent pottery, the best thing about Mollie was her prose. Here are the first paragraphs of *Daddy For Sale*.

> *I hear my Daddy tell my Mama to damn well keep his little girl Maggie—that's me—away from that queer Goofy John because he's not only six shingles short of a shed roof, he's a goddam pervert.*
>
> *Mama says Daddy shouldn't say such things about the poor man, a disabled veteran like that, whose lungs had*

been gassed up with mustard in the Great War. She's sure he wouldn't harm a fly.

So Daddy cusses a few bad words and says, my God, woman! Don't you understand what I'm saying? Don't you know what he is?

And she says, of course she knows, everyone knows he's some kind of artist who makes those little seashell dolls he sells to the tourists who come to Nye Beach, and Fern says he also used to be an officer in the army, which is why he dresses like that, and yes, John is a little peculiar, you know, eccentric. He's a loner. Like she said, he's an artist, and aren't artists always a bit different? But mainly, she says, he's suffering from that terrible lung trouble.

Daddy's laugh doesn't sound friendly when he says, oh no, she has it all wrong, and he—Goofy—doesn't have him, my Daddy, fooled for a minute. He's just a goddam pansy, that's all there is to it!

Mollie was a dynamic kick-ass woman, and an inspiration. Here is her obituary.

> ***Mollie Poupeney*** *(1926-2002)—passed away peacefully on April 30, 2002. Beloved wife of 53 years of Leon Poupeney; loving mother of Mardi Treanor; Paddy and David Poupeney; and cherished grandmother. A memorial service was held on June 14, 2002.*

Chapter 20

A Comedy of Errol's
Dakin Matthews

The U.S. economy in the early '70s suffered a big dip. There was a recession *and* a stock market crash. This was during the Nixon presidency, which was a disaster in itself.

All of this affected advertising, but we were lucky; in the late 1970's Ed was hired by an ad man in Fresno to do a series of farmers' portraits for Bank of America. For a year, Ed and George Thomas traveled on auto trips through the rich and fertile valleys of California, Ed photographing and George interviewing almond growers, vegetable and fruit growers, wheat and rice farmers, etc.

Ed did the series of illustrations in his studio at home, and the ads ran for two years in agriculture journals and magazines.

On the home front, our teenage daughter had begun to attract boys, and she 'went steady' with several. We made an effort to discourage this serious dating, and as a result she became increasingly moody and uncooperative. I compared notes with friends, and their experiences in rearing teenage daughters were pretty much the same. In the meantime, our shy son had surprisingly become a big success in high school theatrics, and we were overjoyed when he was accepted into the Theater Arts Department at UCLA.

When we heard what had happened to our friends the Moxleys, any problems we had with our own kids melted away. The family had moved east. Dave, a brilliant fellow, had moved higher up in his accounting firm. Their future looked rosy, but in 1975, inside a gated community in Greenwich, Connecticut, their daughter Martha was murdered.

She was fifteen.

After the funeral, along with Ed, the Meins and Kenneth Derrs, I went back to be with Dorthy and Dave. They were outwardly stoic, but utterly heartbroken, of course. I'll never forget their bravery in the face of the tragedy. Since the murderer turned out to be Ethel Kennedy's nephew, the publicity went on for many years, and there was one trial heaped upon another.

Dave passed away thirteen years after the murder, but Dorthy carried on with the help of son John and her own wide and loving circle of friends. Dominick Dunne wrote a fictionalized version of the story, *A Season in Purgatory*, filmed for television. There were other books, a plethora of articles, and Dorthy, anxious to keep the case in front of the public until it was solved, became a fixture on many news shows of the day. She was always brave, always open about her feelings, never maudlin.

One of the ways she coped during those years was by making necklaces for her friends, using buttons, charms, and old coins. This required a great deal of craftsmanship, and all her pieces bore the mark of her flawless taste. Through the years I received several. One is in silver, a large pierced heart surrounded by old silver coins and charms from my childhood bracelet: the tiny Eiffel Tower, plump Jimmy Jeffries heart, and miniature piano. Once Dorthy and I were in an elevator at the Metropolitan Museum, and a stranger commented on it.

"*She* made it!" I said, tapping Dorthy's arm.

I never wear one of her necklaces without thinking of her, and a rush of her bravery transfers directly from the necklace to me.

It was 1979, and for two reasons, I needed to go back to college.

One, I needed employment. With our son soon to leave for UCLA and our daughter going to college in another three years, finances were tight. I tried several office jobs, but none were challenging enough or offered much money. I vowed never to teach junior high school again, but maybe if I got my secondary credential and could teach in high school, or if I was able to attain a master's degree and be hired at junior college level, I could earn a decent salary.

Two, besides needing to work, I was dying to do more literary studies. I was pretty sure English credits would apply toward a secondary teaching credential, so I checked with the Department of Education in Sacramento, and they assured me that they would.

I enrolled at Cal State Hayward, a forty-minute drive from Lafayette, and commuted to Hayward three times a week for two years. I took classes in poetry, grammar, literature, and theater arts. I loved all the classes, even Chaucer, and I especially liked my Shakespeare professor, Dakin Matthews, who was self-deprecating and funny, and who had an impressive background as an Elizabethan scholar.

In my second year, there were probably twenty or so students in Dakin's advanced Shakespeare class. We were all older than the average student, and I was the oldest of all.

One of the segments of our class was learning to direct. Matthews assigned one of Shakespeare's plays to each of us and told us to choose a scene, organize a cast, and perform it in class.

I drew *Othello,* and was pleased because I had seen the play twice, once at the Zellerbach Theater in Berkeley and once on television, the Lawrence Olivier version. We were to work on our scenes during the second half of the two-hour class. Our performances would be spread over the semester, and would count for one-third of our grade.

I turned in a paper stating I intended to direct a brief version of Act V, Scene II, when Othello murders Desdemona. I asked Errol Harris, an African-American classmate, to be my Othello, and he said he'd be happy to do it. Errol had a great, deep-timbered voice—how lucky could I get? For Desdemona, I asked Norma Davis, a pretty blonde theater major; and for Emilia I tried a succession of women. Each had already been booked, so I approached Betsy Randall, a flighty redhead who always seemed to be two steps behind. No matter, Emilia had only a few lines, when she broke in at the end of the murder scene.

Our group was to perform two weeks hence, so through the theater department I reserved a small couch; a long brocade robe for Othello; and a skirt, bodice, and laced vest for Emilia. For a touch of opulence, I bought a long rope of pearls for Desdemona. Norma said she would supply her own gown, and I planned to bring a sofa cushion from home for the murder weapon.

Then Katy came down with mononucleosis, and I stayed home with her for a week. Luckily, I had Errol's phone number, and I asked him to take over rehearsals. He did, phoning me regularly to report on how things were going. Unfortunately, I was able to direct the scene only once before the performance.

When the day arrived, I was jumpy and tense, though certain we would put on the most outstanding performance of the day. My actors were very good, though Betsy/Emilia was a bit stilted and unsure of herself. Our scene was to follow two other student-directed scenes: one from *Romeo and Juliet*, and another from *As You Like It*.

I thought their scenes were mediocre—surely we would top them. Even though I hadn't been in charge all the way, we'd had the advantage of many rehearsals. *What could go wrong?*

Errol and another fellow carried in the sofa and placed it at the front of the classroom. Desdemona/Norma lay down, feigning sleep, and Othello/Errol entered and began to deliver his lines.

They finished the section where Desdemona says she can't believe Othello means to kill her—*what has she done to deserve this!*

Then:

DESDEMONA	*O, banish me, my lord, but kill me not!*
OTHELLO	*Down, strumpet!*
DESDEMONA	*Kill me to-morrow: let me live to-night!*
OTHELLO	*Nay, if you strive--*
DESDEMONA	*But half an hour!*
OTHELLO	*Being done, there is no pause.*
DESDEMONA	*But while I say one prayer!*
OTHELLO	*It is too late.*

(He stifles her)

Then—*real* tragedy! As Errol pressed the cushion into Norma's face, he caught his thumb in her necklace. He jerked it away, the string broke, and a cascade of pearls streamed onto the bare floor, where they began to bounce in all directions.

The contrast between the flowery language and the silly accident was ludicrous, and the scene became farce verging on slapstick. The class began to chuckle, then to laugh out loud.

I stole a glance at Professor Matthews, and he was laughing, too!

Now Emilia entered and began her lines:

EMILIA	*Out, and alas! that was my lady's voice.*
	Help! help, ho! help! O lady, speak again!
	Sweet Desdemona! O sweet mistress, speak!
DESDEMONA	*A guiltless death I die.*
EMILIA	*O, who hath done this deed?*
DESDEMONA	*Nobody; I myself. Farewell*
	Commend me to my kind lord: O, farewell!
[Dies]	
OTHELLO	*Why, how should she be murder'd?*
EMILIA	*Alas, who knows?*

I had never realized how squeaky Betsy's voice was, or how many *'uh's'* she could manage to insert into her lines.

"O—*uh*—who hath done—*uh*—this—*uh*—deed?" and "*Uh*—alas—*uh*—who knows?"

I wanted to walk out the door and never return, but at last the scene came to a close. Desdemona swooned for the second time and fell back, dead at last, and the class began to clap with joy that it was over.

I joined the cast at the front of the room, and we took our bows. There was more clapping, but I was sure it was pity applause.

Fifteen minutes later, after the class had filed out, Matthews sat on at his desk, shuffling papers, and I was still gathering up pearls. I didn't have a broom or a brush, and had to collect one frigging pearl at a time.

Why didn't he leave! Didn't he have to be someplace else? Usually he high-tailed it out of there as soon as class was over. Finally, after clearing his throat, he spoke.

"I have to congratulate you, Mrs. Diffenderfer. It seems you have made a comedy out of one of the world's greatest tragedies."

He was grinning, and I managed a sickly smile. For once, I couldn't think of anything to say.

At the end of the semester Matthews gave me an A, and I could only assume it was for extreme valor in the face of mortification.

After he left Hayward, and a few years after I took his classes, Dakin Matthews began having tremendous success in Hollywood as a character actor, appearing in countless films. He was in Steven Spielberg's *Lincoln*, and he played Judge Byers in *Bridge of Spies*. My favorite role of Dakin's is as Colonel Stonehill in *True Grit*, where in a great comedic scene he is out-horse-traded by Haley Steinfeld.

You can catch him on YouTube, singing, in the Broadway musical *Waitress*.

I couldn't believe that until I heard it.

I never got my master's degree, because the language requirements buffaloed me. No doubt I could've brought my college French up to snuff, but a second language was required, Italian or German, and I knew I wasn't up to that. Besides, family problems had intervened.

However, with nose to grindstone, I fulfilled the requirements for a high school English credential, and soon got a job teaching English and Theater Arts at a high school forty minutes from my home.

***Dakin Matthews** (1940-   ) born in Oakland, began his stage career in 1965 in the San Francisco Bay Area, appearing in both Marin and California Shakespeare Festivals, and becoming a member of American Conservatory Theatre. He has made many guest appearances on television, and appeared in more than 25 feature films, including* Nuts, Like Father Like Son, Clean and Sober, Thirteen Days, Child's Play 3, Funny Farm, True Grit *(as Colonel Stonehill) and Steven Spielberg's* Lincoln. *As a stage actor, he's known for his Shakespearean roles, especially King Lear, Bottom, and Falstaff, and most recently for portrayals of C. S. Lewis in South Coast Repertory's* Shadowlands, *as "Warwick" in* Henry IV *at Lincoln Center Theater, also Falstaff, King Lear, and Bottom.*

He appeared in Major Barbara *and* Misalliance *for South Coast Repertory, in Shakespeare Center L.A.'s production of* Much Ado About Nothing, *in* A Man For All Seasons *at the Roundabout, and as "Senator Carlin" in Gore Vidal's* The Best Man *on Broadway. In 2010, Matthews joined the cast of ABC's* General

Hospital as Judge Peter Carroll. He is also a playwright, director, and theater scholar who has published books and articles on Shakespeare and translations of 17th-century Spanish theater. He has been a dramaturg on many theatrical productions, including the 2005 Broadway revival of Julius Caesar starring Denzel Washington, and the 2003 revival of Henry IV, winning a Drama Desk Award Special Award for his adaptation of the latter.

Matthews was Artistic Director of Berkeley Shakespeare Festival, California Actors Theatre, The Antaeus Company (which he co-founded), and Andak Stage Company; he is an Associate Artist of the Old Globe Theatre, and a founding member of the John Houseman's The Acting Company. He appeared as "Richard Russell" in the award-winning L.B.J. play All The Way, starring Bryan Cranston at A.R.T. in Cambridge. Matthews appeared in the Broadway musical Rocky the Musical in 2014, and in 2015, played Winston Churchill opposite Helen Mirren as Queen Elizabeth II in The Audience on Broadway. Matthews portrayed Judge Byers in the 2015 film Bridge of Spies.

Chapter 21

'Age, I Do Abhor Thee' [1]
Mercedes Ruehl

After he graduated from UCLA's Department of Theater, Craig became part of a repertory company in Santa Maria, California. It was called PCPA, for Pacific Conservatory of the Performing Arts, and was located halfway between Santa Barbara and San Luis Obispo. The work was challenging enough to keep Craig on his toes, and he had good roles in important plays over a period of five years.

Like our son, most of the actors and actresses were very young.

The company was currently doing George Bernard Shaw's *Misalliance,* set in 1910 at an English lord's country

---

[1] 'Age, I do abhor thee; youth, I do adore thee' is a line from an anthology of poems, *The Passionate Pilgrim*, 20 poems attributed to Shakespeare and published in 1599.

home. Craig was playing the airplane pilot who crashes on the estate, and the actress Mercedes Ruehl was playing the glamorous circus acrobat who crashes with him.

Ms. Ruehl's appearance probably sold quite a few tickets. It was the eighties, and we had seen her in a number of films. I think this may have been after *Charing Cross Road* and before *Big*.

Ed and I drove down to see the play. I've always loved Shaw's wordiness, and this time his words were mostly a debate about marriage. There are *eight* marriage proposals offered during the course of one play! A male character utters Shaw's famous theory:

> *If marriages were made by putting all the men's names into one sack and the women's names into another, and having them taken out by a blind-folded child, like lottery numbers, there would be just as high a percentage of happy marriages as we have now.*

We always went backstage after one of Craig's plays, and in those years I don't think he minded. We still thought of him as our kid, and I guess that's how he thought of himself. We greeted Craig, then Mercedes, who was leaning against a wall a little separate from the rest of the cast. Craig introduced us, and we complimented them both on their performances. She was friendly but reserved, and the four of us chatted about the town of Santa Maria and the growth of this mid-coastal area, which was fast becoming a wine center.

Then, as per usual, I opened my mouth one too many times.

"Ms. Ruehl, aren't you a little—" I stopped. I knew enough not to say 'older', but I'd already begun, so I had to go on—"a little more—well—*experienced* than the other actors?"

Her expression had begun to change and by the time I finished, her face was frozen.

Craig stood there, looking helpless. Here was a renowned actress whom he was appearing onstage with, and his mother had just pointed out that she was old! Buried in the question was the hint that her career might be on a downward spiral.

"Oops!" I thought.

After a long pause, Ms. Ruehl recovered from my ham-handed bumbling.

"Uh-m-hm-mm, yes. But I have friends here, and it's great to spend my summer near them."

The embarrassing moment passed. Ed graciously invited her to breakfast with us the next morning. She declined, then turned and found someone else to talk to, and Craig started a conversation with the man who was playing Lord Summerhays. Ed and I went back to our motel.

That was probably the night our son decided his folks shouldn't be part of his backstage experience, and I can't say I blame him.

Believe it or not, this had a happy ending. Next morning, Craig joined us for pancakes at the Santa Maria

Inn. Katy was with us too, having driven up from Santa Barbara, where she was attending junior college. Ed ordered blueberry pancakes, Craig asked for a stack with sour cream and strawberries, and I said I'd have the banana pancakes with maple syrup.

Our daughter, noncommittal as always, muttered, *"Whatever."*

While we were waiting, Mercedes stopped by our table. She said, "I just want you to know, it's been a pleasure acting with your son." Before we could reply, she was gone.

Later on, when Ms. Ruehl was nominated for Best Supporting Actress for *Married to the Mob* and then Best Actress for *The Fisher King*, we were in her corner, and when she won the Academy Award both times, we were as proud as if she had been our own kid . . . or younger sister or . . . *whatever.*

> **Mercedes Ruehl** *(1948-   ) was born in Queens, New York. Her father was of German and Irish descent and her mother of Cuban and Irish ancestry. Ruehl began her career in regional theatre with the Denver Center Theatre Company. Her first starring role on Broadway came in* I'm Not Rappaport. *She went on to win the 1984 Obie Award for her performance in* The Marriage of Bette and Boo *and twenty years later, an Obie for* Woman Before a Glass. *She received a 1991 Tony Award as Best Actress for Neil Simon's* Lost in Yonkers. *She earned two other Tony nominations: in 1995 as Best Actress for a revival of* The Shadow Box, *and in 2002 as Best*

Actress for Edward Albee's *The Goat, or Who is Sylvia?*

Her most acclaimed film role was in *The Fisher King*. Her performance in the film earned her the 1991 Academy Award for Best Supporting Actress, as well as many other awards, including a Golden Globe. Earlier, she won the 1989 National Society of Film Critics Award for Best Supporting Actress for her performance in *Married to the Mob*. She played KACL station manager Kate Costas in five episodes of *Frasier*.

She is the first Cuban-American female Academy Award winner. In 2005, she received the Rita Moreno HOLA Award for Excellence from the Hispanic Organization of Latin Actors. She later played the mother of main character Vincent Chase in HBO's *Entourage*. In 2009, Ruehl returned to the Broadway stage in a production of *The American Plan*. Ruehl next appeared in the drama/horror film *What Ever Happened to Barker Daniels?* In 2012, Ruehl starred in Sarah Treem's play *The How and The Why* at McCarter Theater of Princeton University. In 2018 Ruehl appeared in the role of "Ma" in Harvey Fierstein's revamped and renamed revival of *Torch Song* Off-Broadway.

Chapter 22

Three Years Sitting on a Rock
Mr. Nakamura

When I found a job teaching in high school, I thought, At last! No more of those obnoxious middle-school kids! Now I would be teaching older students who would be sedate, well-mannered, and solicitous of their teacher's every wish.

Wrong!

My new job was instructing English and Drama in a large high school located a long way from my house. It was a forty-minute commute, but I would be getting a good salary; that is, for teachers. The job was in an agricultural community, now becoming more citified. The students were from farming families, townsfolk, Mexican laborers, and prosperous boating families with homes on Discovery Bay—a whole truckload of diversity. We had a small proportion of African American students as well.

I soon found that, like always, I would have problems with discipline. There were many small and soul-trying incidents all nine months, but the biggest problem arose when my drama students put on the annual play in May. I chose Eugene O'Neill's *Ah Wilderness!* and the kids seemed to really enjoy rehearsals.

An early problem arose with casting, when a talented black kid tried out for the lead part of Richard, and I chose a white student instead. Oliver (not his real name) was very angry, and confronted me. Feeling guilty, I was defensive, but managed to get over the hump.

The crisis came on our big night, our *only* night, when some of my crew of young actors and actresses were caught drinking. I knew nothing of this, but somehow got the blame.

I was fired at the end of the school year.

I was crestfallen, humiliated. Angry, too, because I had worked so hard, grading papers into the wee hours; giving exams, putting everything I had into a very tough job. The only consolation was that the principal and the District Superintendent of Schools were fired also. Looking back, I think the school board was cutting costs. With my nine years of teaching, I was drawing a much bigger salary than the young man who replaced me could earn.

I decided that teaching wasn't for me. After I got fired, or not rehired, as Ed liked to phrase it, something happened that lifted my spirits. Ed's cousin Barbara Thompson and her husband Rich invited us to Peoria, where they'd moved for his job with Caterpillar. With them, we did a side trip to Chicago for a performance of *Mamma Mia!* and some very expensive martinis—all a lot of fun. Ed was getting bigger commissions now, and I decided I wouldn't go back to work.

As usual, I needed to find an outlet for my creative energy. Through my friend Joyce Blegen, I learned that Maj-Britt Hilstrom in El Cerrito headed a group of women printmakers called the Blue Bay Press. Joyce, an immensely talented woman, was already in the group, and since I had studied printmaking in college and was a working portrait artist, I was invited in.

I was thrilled because this had come just at the right time in my life.

We met twice a week, paying our leader a monthly fee for the privilege of using her printing press. Like me, Maj-Britt had no separate studio, but had converted her large family room for that use. We were all doing monotypes, and Maj-Britt explained that she wasn't our teacher, but only providing a place for us to work.

Monotype is a very old art form. Mono means 'one'; instead of serial printing like lithography, etching, serigraph, etc., only one print is made. Degas and Gauguin worked in the medium, and two California painters, Wayne Thiebaud and Ed's friend Nathan Oliviera, head of printmaking at Stanford, were masters of the technique.

Joyce and I traveled to El Cerrito twice a week for eight years, and during that time we were all very prolific. Joyce and Maj-Britt were not alone in being talented, hard-working artists—Frankie Gilmour, Virginia Munroe, Joan Finton, and Wanda Ultan were of equal ability.

We got to be great friends, and had many potluck parties, with husbands included. Virginia's husband, Joe Munroe, was a nationally-known photographer who had photographed Georgia O'Keefe, and had done the famous photo of college kids stuffed in a phone booth.

Maj-Britt was the sparkplug who made connections for several group shows. We even had a show in Southern California at California State College in Fullerton, where we showed some impressively large works our leader dubbed 'magnatypes'. They were 40" x 60", and all were diptychs; we used two 30" x 40" sheets of paper joined together, to create them. Since we all had such different styles, there was a great deal of diversity in our output. I was designated as the landscapist and, as I recall, my prints were the only magnatypes verging on realism.

I called them abstract landscapes, a category I did not invent.

After eight years of printmaking two days a week, I had a huge body of work I wanted to show and possibly sell, so I made a connection with the American Society of Architects and obtained permission to have a show in their downtown Oakland showroom. The opening was a big night in my life, with friends and family members attending. Both Craig and Katy were there, and I made a few sales.

So why stop there?

I decided to try for San Francisco. But I had no entree; I wasn't a well-known artist, and no prominent gallery was interested in my work. I'd been using a framer on Clement Street in the City for the last four years, and the owner operated an art gallery as an auxiliary to his business.

Clement is in the Inner Richmond District, not far from Geary Boulevard. It's a busy, thriving neighborhood, with many restaurants and shops.

Mr. Nakamura, owner of the framing shop, was a small man, a gentle soul with a wry take on life. He was friendly and outgoing, specializing in Japanese proverbs which always struck my funny bone.

One day I asked, "Mr. Nakamura, do you think I could ever have a show of my monotypes in your gallery?"

"Of course!" he said, making a little bow. I signed a contract in which I promised to pay 5% of any sales. It was August, and since he already had other shows scheduled, we settled on the date of October 15th.

Chatting away as usual, I mentioned that on the way there, I had been shocked to see several buildings with graffiti spray-painted on their sides.

"And some kids think it's art!" I fumed.

"The moon and the Chinese soft-shelled turtle," murmured Mr. Nakamura.

"And that means?"

His young assistant Hildy answered for him. "Both are round, but their worth is very different."

"Oh," I said.

Even after receiving an explanation, these inscrutable sayings usually made sense to me many hours later.

I made arrangements with a printer for mailers, a glossy postcard with date, time, and place on one side and one of my prints on the reverse. The next time I went back to measure the walls, I confided that I hoped the show would help my sales, and that even though I was currently showing my work in two separate venues in Walnut Creek and Lafayette, I hadn't sold anything in four months.

"Three years sitting on a rock," he said.

I had to ask.

"You know what happens when you sit on a rock?" he said. "It gets warm. So even though you are going through hard times, things will get better."

"I sure hope so!"

At home, I started selecting the pieces I wanted to show. It was a small gallery, but I thought it was big enough to show twelve 20 x 30's and two 30 x 40's. No magnatypes, they were too big.

I asked Ed to help me choose. His style was much more realistic than mine, but he seemed to admire my loose approach, and had always been encouraging about my art career.

The second week of October, Hildy and I hung the show. Hildy was second-generation Japanese, or Nisei, and a modern American girl in every way. She wore stripes a lot; even her spectacle frames were striped, and that day her stockings were a startling combination of fuchsia and florescent-green.

I brought out my tools, a large screwdriver and a tiny claw hammer. Mr. Nakamura was standing nearby, and I heard him say, *"Too long for an obi, too short for a tasuki."*

Aha! I got the gist of that one.

"I don't know where Ed keeps all his tools, but won't these do?"

"Don't think so," said Hildy, producing a large hammer which looked much more efficient than mine.

After a couple of hours' work, measuring, hanging and re-hanging, I moaned, "I hope this is going to be worth it!"

I was struggling to support one end of a magnatype, with Mr. Nakamura holding the other end, while Hildy stood off to one side to see if we'd chosen the right spot. I had changed my mind about showing such a large piece, and had put a high price on it, $3000. Who knew? Maybe it would sell.

"Jumping off from the Kiyomizu stage," said Mr. Nakamura.

"What does *that* mean?"

He explained that this was the observation deck at the Kiyumizo temple in Kyoto, but that didn't help me understand.

"Just take the plunge and hope for the best," translated Hildy, grinning.

At the end of the day, while gathering up my things, I confided to Mr. Nakamura, "I might as well not invite my friends. I think they're tired of coming to my shows, and they never buy anything!"

"Chanting a prayer to Buddha into a horse's ear," he quoted. "Some people do not appreciate art. But do not worry. Be quiet in your soul, and try to relax."

"That's great advice, I'll try to follow it," I said, patting him on the shoulder on my way out.

On the second day of hanging, I said, "Mr. Nakamura, I'm so grateful! Let me take you to lunch. I saw a Chinese place just two doors away, will that do?"

He hemmed and hawed, then relented. As we sat over egg rolls and fried rice, for some reason I started talking about my children.

"My daughter is tied up with a guy who doesn't work," I moaned, "and our son is barely surviving as an actor. Along with that, I'm pretty sure they both smoke pot!"

Mr. Nakamura poured more tea.

"Without knowing, you can be at peace like Buddha."

"You mean ignorance is bliss?" He nodded, and we went back to the egg rolls. I was beginning to catch on.

Finally October 15th arrived, and Ed and I got there early. The show went beautifully, and many of my friends showed up. At that time Craig was in repertory theater in Denver, and Katy was at home in Emeryville, but many habitues of Clement Street dropped in to take a look at the art. One of the local Chinese restauranteurs bought the magnatype, and I made five other sales. Ron and Lorrie Gazzano bought a piece, and so did my friend Carmella

Smith. Chuck Lawrence's wealthy wife Marge from Dallas bought two pieces, an abstract and a landscape.

This cheered me up. I gave most of the money to Ed for our bank account, sent my kids a check for a hundred each, then splurged on a new leather jacket.

Everyone in the Bay Area has a story about the Loma Prieta earthquake of 1989, and Ed and I, too, have a story.

The quake occurred two days after my show, on October 17 at 5:04 p.m. The shaking lasted for only 20 seconds, but with a magnitude of 6.9, the shock was responsible for 63 deaths and 3,757 injuries. Because it happened during a live broadcast of the World Series between the San Francisco Giants and the Oakland Athletics, it's sometimes referred to as the "World Series earthquake".

Rush-hour traffic on the freeways was lighter than normal because the game at Candlestick Park was about to begin, and this probably prevented a larger loss of life.

We were on our way across the Bay Bridge to the Opera House, but were listening on the car radio to the game. Jeff Meyers, a friend of Ed's, had given us tickets to *Imonedeo*. I hadn't heard of that opera, but I was never one to turn up my nose at free tickets.

We weren't far from the toll gate when suddenly the radio went out.

What was this! At the same moment I saw a big wave of water rise to the right of our car. Months later I learned there had been a small tsunami near the shore of Monterey Bay. Due to the movement of the car, we hadn't felt a thing.

In a few seconds the radio came back on, and an excited announcer announced that we'd had an earthquake. It was Al Michaels at Candlestick, sounding breathless and worried. We pulled up to the tollgate, where a heavy black woman was collecting tolls. I don't think she had a clue about what had happened.

My teasing husband handed over the money and asked, "Was it good for you?"

The woman gave him a puzzled look, but took his money. Maybe she'd never heard the joke, or hadn't felt any movement, or both. She was as uncomprehending as we were about the huge catastrophe that had just occurred.

We drove through the tollgate, but were soon halted by one of the heroes of the moment, a young man who stood in the middle of the roadway stopping cars and signaling for everyone to make a U-turn and go back.

The Bay Bridge had collapsed!

Ed was outwardly calm, but I was in a state of panic. I wanted to stop in Emeryville, where Katy was living with our grandchild, three-year-old Alex. No, Ed said, we're going home.

It was just as well, because Katy and Ricardo, carrying Alex, were walking on MacArthur Boulevard in Oakland when the earthquake struck. They heard the Nimitz freeway fall, and they said it made a frightening, thunderous sound, echoing for miles.

Forty-two deaths occurred with the collapse of the upper level of a double-deck portion of the freeway, crushing the cars on the lower level, and causing crashes on the upper level. It was horrendous!

We finally arrived home, where we found that the only change was that one of our Gold Country wooden candlesticks next to the fireplace had toppled over on its side. Its mate, flanking the other side, was still upright.

Months later, when the *San Francisco Chronicle* ran a contest asking for stories about the event, I sent in a poem about our experience and won dinner for two at a San Francisco restaurant. I've forgotten the name of the place, but there must have been a ceremony, because Gavin Newsom was there with Kimberly Guilfoyle.

Nobody bothered with Ed and me. That was fine with us, in a booth chomping away on veal piccata.

Three days after the catastrophe, Ed and I went to retrieve my unsold monotypes from the framing shop. We had to take both the San Rafael and the Golden Gate bridges to get to the city, and it took forever.

Mr. Nakamura seemed distraught, but I think he was more concerned about his neighboring shopkeeper's damage than his own. Both his windows were destroyed, one shattered, the other cracked but still in place, and much of the pottery he'd been displaying for a ceramist was still littering the floor.

He said his sister's home had been destroyed, and that she was in the hospital with two broken legs. We told him of our experience approaching the bridge.

Naturally, he had a proverb. As Ed stood at the door holding the first load of my unsold works, I stood near Mr. Nakamura with my arm through his. I'll never forget the expression on his face; calm, heavy-hearted and determined all at the same time.

"*My barn having burned down, I can now see the moon,*" he said.

Mr. Nakamura is the only fictional character in this memoir. His gallery and the art show are a fusion of the many experiences I had during the years I spent promoting my monotypes.

Chapter 23

"Hey, Vernon!"
Vernon Alley

I was leafing through *Vogue* at the hairdresser's one day when I happened to see an article about a model named Aleece Wilson. She was quoted as saying how proud she is of her freckles.

"In past times," she said, "everybody hid their freckles. Now I get jobs because I have them!"

There were pictures of other models, all extolling their own little brown spots, and as I sat there sipping coffee and reading, my memory went back to something that happened to me in the sixties.

I first caught sight of Vernon Alley when he was playing string bass at Barnaby Conrad's Matador Café in San Francisco. We were sitting at a table near the musicians, and when Ed hailed Vernon, he waved back with a big smile.

Vernon smiled at everybody. A stocky, middle-aged black man, he spent his early years playing and traveling with Count Basie and Duke Ellington, but decided that the life wasn't for him, so he moved back to the Bay Area.

Ed knew him at the Bohemian Club. Vernon was the club's first black member, and his friend Noah Griffin said that, soon after joining, Vernon was the most popular member of the club.

The Vernon Alley Trio was a fixture on San Francisco's nightlife scene, not just at the Matador, but anywhere jazz was played. He served as musical director of the Blackhawk for years, where he played with the biggest jazz names, Charlie Parker among them. Vernon worked hard to integrate the Musician's Union and to break down color barriers in San Francisco jazz.

He eventually got into city politics, and was chosen to serve on the San Francisco Arts Commission and the Human Rights Commission.

In the late '60s, a few wealthy Manhattan Bohemians gave a party at the Waldorf Astoria, and they flew some of the club's band members and their wives back to New York to entertain. This included Ed and me. After the party, followed by a jam session at a millionaire's apartment on Sutton Place, Vernon, Ed, and I ended up at the Café Carlyle listening to Bobby Short. Bobby was a friend of Vernon's, and after they greeted one another across the room, Vernon said, "Watch out! When he comes over, he'll want to kiss me."

Bobby did seem overjoyed to see Vernon, although no kissing occurred, and he was gracious to Ed and me as well. I could have cared less whether the famous pianist was gay or straight—I thought he was the greatest entertainer I'd ever heard. I loved everything about Bobby: his polished, urbane look, his piano technique and intimate singing style, his warm personality. I was sure it wasn't just his musical chops but also his teddy-bear persona that got him where he was. (Years later I ran into him at the Big Four, a restaurant on Nob Hill. He greeted me warmly, pretending to remember me, though I'm sure he didn't. Either way, my women friends were mightily impressed.)

It was that bar-hopping night in New York when I unwittingly said something that angered Vernon. The three of us were drinking and had been drinking for some time, while my mom twirled in her grave. It was very late, and sitting at a tiny table, chin balanced on one hand, I asked, "Vernon, how come you have freckles?"

He was a light-colored black man, and the spots on his face were very prominent. I had freckles as a child, and they vanished in my teens, so I wondered why Vernon still had his.

All at once, he got up from the table and left without a word.

"*Oh!*" I said to Ed. "Why'd he take offense at *that!*"

He didn't answer. I think he was as puzzled as I was.

Back home in Oakland, when I recalled the incident, I was overcome with remorse. Here was a musician friend of my husband's, one of the very few black members of his club, and I had somehow insulted him.

I asked Ed several times, "Do you think I should call and say I'm sorry?" but he told me to put it out of my mind.

Months passed, maybe a year, and one evening we were in San Francisco. I spotted Vernon across the room, walked over, and said, "Vernon, I'm so sorry if I offended you that time in New York. I felt terrible about it!"

"Forget it." He grinned and touched my arm. "I was drunk."

Just then a woman friend pulled me aside and asked how to find the Ladies Room, and I didn't have a chance to talk to him again that night—or ever.

In the decades to follow, Vernon went through some terrible times with bad health, and due to his diabetes, had to have a leg amputated. In 2001, friends gave him a three-hour tribute, "The Legacy of Vernon Alley." We were in Texas and couldn't go, but we heard that it drew almost a thousand musicians and friends, and when he walked onstage, there was a standing ovation. Vernon's girlfriend, Lorna deRuyter, was quoted as saying that the tribute was very important to him, but that his friends were worried he wouldn't make it. Somehow, despite everything, he played several numbers, including "Big Fat Butterfly," his signature tune for 60 years.

In 2004, Vernon died. A memorial service was held at Grace Cathedral on Nob Hill, and hundreds of the city's prominent folks in politics and music showed up to honor him. As we drove over the Bay Bridge to the service, Ed told me a story I'd never heard.

Ed, Ken McCaulou, Carl Eberhard, and Vernon were playing a gig at a Rotary luncheon in Orinda, a suburb of Oakland. Carl, a composer as well as a brilliant pianist, had written "A History of Jazz" set to music, and that's what the fellows performed. Ed said that Vernon, when introduced to the Rotarians, got more applause and shouts of recognition than anyone else.

When Vernon was ready to leave, his car wouldn't start, so he had it towed to the nearest corner gas station. While the musicians were standing around with him, waiting for a new battery to be installed, a garbage truck drove by with two black fellows hanging on the side.

"*Hey, Vernon!*" one yelled, and Vernon yelled back, "Hey, man!"

Ed and Ken and Carl laughed their heads off. You couldn't go anywhere where Vernon wasn't known, not even lily-white Orinda and its garbage truck guys.

We parked on Nob Hill, and when we walked through the mammoth bronze doors of the cathedral, a huge crowd had already gathered. Ed and I were in our seventies and were losing our hearing—Ed because the brass section blaring in his ears for decades, and both because of age. In order not to miss anything, we walked down the aisle to one of the front rows.

It was an unusual service. There were countless eulogies from city fathers and musicians, and a jazz quintet perched in a special niche near the podium, playing between all the accolades. An hour of speeches went by, and Nancy Pelosi, House Democratic Minority Leader of Congress and native of the city, spoke last. She gave an affectionate and inspiring speech, emphasizing Vernon's important role in city race relations. Her words were very moving, and when she finished, in an excess of emotion I turned to the woman next to me and said, "Wasn't that *wonderful?*"

Until that moment, I never knew what the term 'fish-eye' meant. The woman gave me such a look of disapproval that I was chilled to the bone.

Did I offend her by talking at such a solemn occasion? Or was I being impertinent by merely speaking to her?

Maybe she hated Nancy Pelosi's guts!

Suddenly, I realized who the woman was. I was sitting next to Charlotte Mailliard, one of the leading social arbiters of San Francisco, married to a dedicated and distinguished Republican, George Shultz, on her other side,

I wanted to give her a sharp elbow to the ribs, but then the organ music soared, and Ed and I began to walk arm-in-arm up the aisle. We found our car and drove to Vernon's wake at Moose's Restaurant in Washington Square. There, to a packed, standing-room-only crowd, a piano, tenor sax, drums, trombone, and bass played a tribute to the great jazz man. Dozens of musicians took turns, and the session lasted for hours.

Nancy Pelosi was there, but the Schultzes did not attend.

> *Vernon Alley (1915–2004) was an American jazz bassist and the most distinguished jazz musician in San Francisco history. A man who broke down many racial barriers in his lifetime and played with the greatest musicians of his generation, Alley could have become one of the most famous names in jazz, but chose to spend his career in his hometown. He went to New York in 1940 and joined the Lionel Hampton band, moving later to the Count Basie Orchestra. He was at the pinnacle of the jazz world at the age of 27. He and Baby, his bass, jammed with almost all the great jazz musicians and singers of the 20th century.*
>
> *He became a part of city lore, publicized by the late Herb Caen, and perhaps the most loved man who ever be-bopped in San Francisco. Like most black men of his era, Alley struggled against racism to get where he was, almost single-handedly integrating the city's musician unions and breaking a color line outside the Fillmore District. When Las Vegas casinos forced black musicians to enter through back doors, Alley joined a fight to end institutionalized bigotry. But it was Alley's twinkling eye and booming infectious laugh that broke down barriers.*
>
> *In the late 1930's, Alley was a regular player at clubs in San Francisco. The music scene would explode in the 1940's when thousands of African Americans moved*

to the Bay Area to work in the shipyards. Musicians came from everywhere to play San Francisco clubs, and such immortals as Lionel Hampton, Coleman Hawkins, and Dizzy Gillespie joined Alley's trio for jam sessions. In Las Vegas, Alley had another bitter taste of racism. In the '40s and '50s, even Ella Fitzgerald had to use the back door at casinos in Las Vegas, known then by African Americans as "the Mississippi of the West." Alley was infuriated when prevented from visiting old football teammates staying where he and Fitzgerald were playing. At a musicians' union convention in Philadelphia, he railed against what he called "the most bigoted place in the world," telling the Las Vegas contingent, "I will never again go any place where I cannot walk through the front door." In 1960, the casino owners finally caved after threatened with a protest march.

In 1974 he became the first black man to be accepted into the exclusive Bohemian Club. He said it was a membership he was proud of because of the many talented musicians, artists, and all-around good people in the club. He refused to be the token black, demanding that the club also bring in his friend, pianist John Horton Cooper. Noah Griffin, also a Bohemian, said Alley soon became the most popular man in the club. There is a portrait of him by Joe Cleary, smiling and holding his bass, in the Cartoon Room of the club's San Francisco building.

Alley's popularity extended across San Francisco. When he walked into a bar, ten people shouted his name. Mayor Willie Brown, on the list of 'Who's Who' of San Francisco, called Alley a friend, and Herb Caen *never missed an opportunity to mention his old chum "whose smile lights up the town, even on foggy days."*

Chapter 24

Dream Fantasy Finale

One night I had one of those crazy dreams, the kind you have where everything seems so terribly, terribly real. Where you're half awake and want to wake up and get over it.

But this time, I didn't want my dream to end.

It was the middle of August, and I'd finished my vignettes about meeting famous people. I sent the manuscript off to my agent, and I must have become attached to my characters and wasn't ready to leave them, because before going to sleep, I began imagining a get-together with everyone I'd written about!

It would be a grand party with all the celebrities there—the dead ones and those still alive.

Then after I finally dropped off to sleep, a strange thing happened.

It all became real. Or rather, *surreal*.

I sent off invitations through the ether in some unexplained way.

My mind went back and forth. Should I invite Cynthia Mackay? She had been so insulting at that St. Helena party. But my Ed would sorely miss Ed Mackay as his bass player, so I decided to forgive and forget.

My fantasy invitations went out through the air waves, and like lightning slicing through the atmosphere, I got answers back.

Every single character said he or she would like to attend. This was going to be smooth sailing. And what a fantastic array of talent for a party!

Our small house would be way too crowded, so now my yearning for a bigger house came true. Suddenly it was huge, and so was our deck! Our small backyard had been transformed into an enormous area with lawn, garden paths, blooming flowers, picnic tables, and tall trees. This was all so wonderful!

In my delirium, I took two of our pieces down from the living room walls and instead hung Maurice Logan's watercolor and Doel Reed's aquatint.

I intended to do all the cooking, but I would need help, so with my magic powers, I hired two women helpers, one young, one middle-aged. Their names were Sarah and Eloise, and even though their faces were amorphous, I was sure they would anticipate my every wish. I told them that as soon as people arrived to start passing trays of appetizers, and to keep the wine flowing. Naturally, I would provide lovely, expensive wines for our famous guests.

What should I wear? I gazed into a mirror and saw that I was already wearing my usual dress-up outfit, black pants, white blouse, and my Dorthy Moxley necklace with the pierced silver heart.

The doorbell rang, and Mollie Poupeney was at the door.

She looked the same, like a suburban hippie, wearing chinos and a faded sweatshirt. Her brown eyes shone with excitement, and the halo of grey-brown curls circling her head gave her the appearance of an enchanted seraph.

I gave her a bone-crushing hug.

Ed materialized at my side. I introduced them, then took Mollie aside and said, "I want to ask you something. Tell the truth! Do you think I've aged much?"

"Good God in heaven! You're worried about *that*? You've aged less that anyone I know! What I want to ask *you* is, did you finish that book about growing up in the Dust Bowl?"

"Yes. And I know you finished your novel, because I bought it. Well, enjoy the party. And would you do me a favor? If anyone starts to get out of hand, like tries to dominate the gathering or act like a spoiled diva—and Noel Coward might—it's your job to cut them down to size."

"*Noel Coward's coming?* Omigod! Okay, I'll watch out for any oversized egos."

Soon after Mollie came through the door, artist Henry Koerner arrived. He took my hand and said, "How many, many years it has been! And you look just the same!"

"Oh, Henry, I'm so glad you came!"

I'd never called him Henry before, but he didn't seem to mind.

"And is your young student going to be here? Our model, Nessie?"

"Nellie. No, I'm afraid not. And she isn't young anymore, she's a grandmother! No, Henry, I only invited famous people like you."

He smiled, pleased with the compliment, and grabbed a glass of wine off a passing tray.

The doorbell rang again, and I opened the door in time to see a limo pull away.

Vincent Price was here.

I'm sure the actor never knew I existed until he got my invitation, but he was one of the first to arrive.

Go figure.

I turned him over to Ed, because guests were beginning to arrive thick and fast.

When William Scranton appeared, I said, "Governor Scranton, in case you don't know why you've been invited, let me clear that up." I led him into the house. "At the 1964 Republican Convention in San Francisco, my cousin and I were in your delegation marching into the Cow Palace. You marched in with us, remember?"

"Of course I remember! It was one of the most important days of my life! I was in such a state of nerves,

I'm afraid I don't remember you, although I should, you're a pretty girl."

Girl! His eyesight must be failing.

At that moment, Ed hissed in my ear, "You look over-excited—I'm afraid you're going to have one of your spells. How are your knees? Did you take your medications?"

Evidently he was seeing me as I really am—elderly, overweight, with crow's feet and salt-and-pepper hair. On the other hand, I was beginning to realize that my guests and I were the ages we were when we first met.

I ignored Ed as usual and said to Scranton, "Fran and I thought it was so exciting, seeing Eisenhower and Rockefeller and Goldwater! Not to mention all those television journalists."

"*Goldwater!* He would've made a terrible president!"

Scranton screwed up his face as if he were in actual physical pain. "We really dodged the bullet that time!"

He glided away, and at that moment, George and Ellie Shearing arrived. The party was going to be heavy on musicians, but you can never have too many musicians at a party. Ellie gave me a hug, and George said in reply to my question, "Of course I remember you, darling! You laughed at everything I said—I was chuffed! And I felt your face. I do that, don't I, Ellie." His bellowing laugh rang out.

"That's one of your trademarks," said Ellie.

She then led him to our baby grand piano, which used to be an upright.

189

I was overjoyed when Vernon Alley walked in on both legs carrying his big bass fiddle. We hugged, and I reminded him of our bar-hopping night in New York.

"How're your kids?" he asked. "You kept talkin' about 'em."

"I did? Remember? We heard Bobby Short play at the Carlyle, and he came over to our table!"

"Bobby was a great guy. But right now I hear my pal George playin'. See ya!"

With George on piano, Vernon on bass, and Ed on trombone, they began "Take the A Train."

My husband looked as if he'd died and gone to heaven which, in a way, he had.

Next, sidling into the house as if hoping not to be noticed was Mr. Nakamura. I gave him a joyful embrace, then took his arm and ushered him into the room.

"I'm so glad you came!"

"I am pleased to be here." After that, I caught only glimpses of the little man.

When Cynthia arrived with her husband Ed Mackay, she and I acted as if nothing unpleasant had ever occurred between us. We gave each other an air kiss, and I said, "Come in! Glad you can be with us!"

Cynthia looked slim and stylish in dark brown linen, with her usual sprayed bouffant hairdo.

"What is the occasion?" she asked. "You didn't say on the invitation."

"Why does there have to be a. reason for a party!" said Ed. Ed Mackay was always upbeat and jovial when there was a celebration of any kind. And I knew he loved to make music.

"Ed, you'll have to share bass-playing with Vernon Alley. Hope you don't mind."

"Happy to! Makes me glad I didn't lug my instrument along."

I ushered them in, and told them to please introduce themselves.

Just behind the Mackays came Bishop Pike, wearing the same colorful attire as when I first met him, a tunic and purple vest, plus a large gold cross on a heavy gold chain. His eyes, magnified through thick lenses, looked huge.

"We only met once, Bishop—in Marin County at a party. But I'm glad you can be here! I think you'll enjoy the other guests."

"Thank you," he panted. "It was a long drive, and I'm thirsty."

"We have just the thing for that, so come in!"

When I saw tall, mustachioed Melvyn Douglas and Helen Gahagan Douglas at the door, I had to mentally pinch myself. I chatted with them for several minutes, reminding them of Ed's and my backstage visit after his performance in *Inherit the Wind*. Helen Douglas obviously had no memory of the occasion (and I'm not positive he did) but she nodded and smiled.

When I reminded the actor of what he'd said that night, "It's important that young people like you two see this play," his face lit up.

"I'm glad I decided to do that piece of theater. It was, and is, so historically important. But why are we invited here today, young lady?"

"It's like this. I've written stories about everyone you'll see today, people well-known in American culture, and I was dying to get you all together. I know it's a quirky idea, but it's going to be wonderful!"

The Douglases floated into the room.

Next, Maria Tallchief wafted through the door, with George Balanchine following close behind. She looked smashing in a green-and-blue floral dress.

She was immediately pulled away from me by Ellie Shearing, who told her, "I'm such a *fan!*"

I was left with the famous choreographer.

"I don't know if you recall, Mr. Balanchine, but one night at the San Francisco Opera House, some people from Maria's hometown visited her backstage. That was my mother, me, and my husband, who's over there playing trombone. You were so kind, and made us feel welcome. But we were sorry we didn't get to meet Maria."

"I'm afraid I do not remember, please to forgive me. But we are here, so our meeting must have been quite pleasant, no?"

His Russian accent vividly brought back that evening. It had been dark backstage, and in my excitement, I hadn't noticed he was so short. I also hadn't noticed how handsomely Slavic he was, with a sensual mouth and slanted eyes.

At the sound of the doorbell, I moved away.

Xavier Cugat had arrived. He was wearing a tuxedo, red cummerbund, and that ever-present lock of hair dangling over one eye.

"Mr. Cugat! We met way back in the past. Would you believe I was once in a college beauty contest you judged in Stillwater, Oklahoma?"

"*Ha, ha*! Of course!"

His face broadened in an enormous smile, but I could tell he had zero recollection of the event. I went on, hell-bent on making him remember. "I was the last one in the lineup? Wearing a red dress? Abbe Lane helped you judge?"

"Certainly, certainly! Abbe was a wonderful, wonderful girl who I married! We did many, many wonderful shows together—many, many! *Si, si!*"

I gave up.

The doorbell rang, and I greeted Mercedes Ruehl. She looked fabulous, wearing a leopard-print wrap dress topped by a white cashmere stole. Her black hair was very long, her makeup heavy and theatrical.

"Miss Ruehl, how wonderful that you came! I want to remind you of something so you'll know who I am. My husband and I came backstage in Santa Maria when you were acting in *Misalliance* with our son Craig. I'm afraid I said something rude, and you looked so stricken!"

"I remember. But *you* were the one who looked stricken! Don't tell me you've been carrying around guilt all these years!"

She put her hand on my waist and gave it a friendly scrunch. "I loved acting in that Shaw play. D'you know, it's the only play of his I've ever done? But it's never too late!"

She laughed, then turned to Mollie, who was waiting to talk to her.

Ed finally took time out from his trombone to help me welcome people, and we greeted Paul Mills together.

"It's a pleasure to see you two again."

He looked around at the crowd of people, perhaps a bit apprehensive. He was the same as ever, shy and reserved.

"I probably should remind you," I said. "I was in the first class of museum docents, and later on you asked me to take Steven Zellerbach on a private tour."

"I remember you, but not the Zellerbach thing. It was so long ago."

"Sure was! There are several artists coming today, and I hope you get to meet them. You already know Maurice Logan, but I invited one of my art professors, Doel Reed, a southwestern artist known for his lithographs. And Henry Koerner is here. He did a slew of *Time* covers."

"I'll be sure to meet them."

"Let me get you some wine," Ed said, and they walked away together.

Speak of the devil. Steven Zellerbach arrived next, wearing Armani. I had worried he wouldn't know me, but as soon as he stepped inside, he said, "I remember you! You're the young woman who preferred small paintings to big ones."

I laughed. "It's wonderful to see you again!"

When Dakin Matthews arrived, I shook hands way too energetically. He retrieved his hand and stepped back.

"I know you're wondering why I invited you, Dakin, and I'll tell you later. Right now we're heating appetizers, and my oven's not very reliable. Have some wine!"

I got Sarah and Eloise squared away in the kitchen, then came back and found Matthews chatting with Ed. Like a yahoo, I butted in. "I'm glad you two are getting acquainted. Do you remember, Dakin, I was in your advanced Shakespeare class, and you had us directing scenes from his plays."

"Uh-huh. I believe you directed the comedic version of *Othello*."

I laughed.

"You said once that every actor you knew wanted to get in the movies and make a killing. You said it in such a superior way, as if it was something *you* would never do. But that's exactly what you did! Are you ever sorry you went Hollywood?"

He gazed at me, unsmiling. "No, because I'm still doing a lot of stage work. Maybe you haven't heard about that." He was searching the room with his eyes. "Is that Mercedes Ruehl over there?"

"Uh-huh. See you around."

A few minutes later, I was showing Henry Koerner one of my monotypes when Ed rushed over. "Jeanette MacDonald just arrived in a Lincoln Continental, with a driver!"

At the door, Jeanette's reaction to meeting me was smooth as butter.

She said, "Lovely to see you. When I got your invitation I was mystified, but I simply had to come. What an attractive room!"

"I made a fool of myself at breakfast in Las Vegas. I'm almost hoping you don't remember!"

"I think I'm overdressed—I'm so embarrassed!" She was wearing a gorgeous long gown with sparkling diamond earrings.

"Oh no, you're not! I was hoping you would sing for us, so you're dressed perfectly!"

"I would love to sing. Now, let's see if I know anyone here." She donned a dazzling thousand-kilowatt smile, and as she walked into the room, all heads turned.

At that moment Dale Robertson arrived along with Russell Nype, and they were chatting as if they'd known each other forever.

"Russell!" I trilled.

"My *dear!* How wonderful to renew our acquaintance!"

He was even taller than I remembered, and still wearing the same horn-rims. How could a white turtleneck and checked trousers look that good on anyone?

I stood there, mesmerized. Finally I said, "I want us to talk."

He nodded, touching my shoulder before he moved into the room, and Robertson began chatting with Vincent Price.

I needed to take time out. Too much excitement all at once made my palms sweat and my breath come in gasps.

I glanced around. Clumps of celebrities were chatting together, combinations of famous people I could never have imagined. I was in the midst of a dream, but it all seemed so breathtakingly real!

Five minutes later, Ed greeted his old boss Maurice Logan with a clap on the back and a warm hug. Maury, in his late seventies, was still distinguished-looking. Well, of course! He was the same age as when we first met, just like everyone here.

"Red or white wine?" I asked.

He leaned down. "Got anything stronger?"

"Sure!" Ed headed toward the bar.

"I haven't seen you in years!" I said, clasping my hands around his.

"No one has, Missy. I'm pretty much out of the picture. Didn't you come to my funeral?"

"Well, yes, but I wanted to have you back here for this get-together! You're becoming more well-known all the time, Maury. Did you know Nancy Boas and Charles Eldredge wrote a book about the Society of Six?"

"Don't care beans about that old group, just care about my own stuff. Thanks, Ed." He took the highball and downed a big gulp.

It was then that I had another inspiration.

I decided to conjure up Shammy from Dog Heaven!

In a flash, she appeared in all her beagle glory, then had a tail-wagging reunion with Mr. Logan, jumping on him like that other time, except now he was standing up.

Ed was overjoyed to be reunited with our little dog, and the three of them wandered together out to the deck. Maury seemed jollier than I'd ever seen him. Probably had something to do with the whiskey.

Next, Charles Schulz came through the door. He was dressed in a sport shirt and slacks, and was wearing the same shy, ingratiating grin I remembered.

"Welcome, Mr. Schulz! The party seems complete now! I wonder if you remember, I once met you at a golf tournament in Oakland. I was sort of a hostess."

He gazed at me for several seconds. "I remember that I played very badly in that tournament."

"It's such an honor to see you again. Please get some wine, and make yourself at home!"

I was chatting with Governor Scranton when Ed interrupted to tell me that an old man was at the door. I hurried to greet my acquaintance from college days, J. C. Penney. Even though it was a warm summer day, he was wearing a three-piece suit, high collar, and gold watch chain.

"I'm so happy you came, sir! I don't know if you remember me, but I introduced you at a religious event at Oklahoma A & M back in the 1950's. Do you recall?"

His voice was thin and piping. "I'm afraid I don't. I made thousands of talks on college campuses, and now I can't differentiate one from another."

"I used the wrong initials when I introduced you, and was afraid you thought I was making fun."

"Don't remember a thing about it."

"Okay. Well, let's meet some people!"

I started walking him around the room when the doorbell rang again. Ed was playing his horn, so I handed Mr. Penney over to Mollie.

Noel Coward had arrived, wearing a tuxedo and black tie.

I drew him inside, deciding not to mention my near-invasion of his dressing room.

Trembling with both joy and excitement, I said, "We've never met, Mr. Coward, but my husband and I saw your Las Vegas show. It was marvelous—truly a great occasion—and we were blown away!"

I sounded like a whack job, so I stopped and took a deep breath. "I was wondering if you would sing something today."

In mellifluous British tones he replied, "Of course, my dearest, why else would I be here? Incidentally, that Desert Inn show helped me recoup my losses on *Ace of Clubs*. God, what a mistake *that* was! Binky Beaumont in all his years never had such a flop!"

"May I get you some wine? We have red or white."

Coward looked as pained as Scranton had at the mention of Goldwater, but his tortured expression was followed by a look of sympathy.

Poor woman! Such vulgar taste, such lack of discernment! Wine as a cocktail? Really?

"If you would be so kind," he said, "I would like an inordinately dry martini, graced with two large green olives. Then, after you have created it, pour it into a tumbler and add half-again the amount of gin. Thank you so *ve-r-r-ry, ve-r-r-ry* much!"

His eyes, framed by an abundance of laugh wrinkles, looked deeply into mine. Maybe he wasn't such a formidable personage after all.

I led him over to the jazz trio, where he introduced himself. He and Shearing already knew each other, but I watched Vernon's and Ed's jaws drop at the same exact moment.

I hurried away to do the great man's bidding.

I wondered if everyone here was having the same dream I was having.

After delivering the martini to Mr. Coward, I saw Maria talking to Ellie. I looked around, wondering where Balanchine was. There! Standing outside on the deck with Roy Bogas. I walked out and found that they were deep into a discussion of Russian composers.

When Roy arrived, he said he didn't remember me, even though I prodded him with that pathetic artichoke story. He did remember eating at the Chateau de Longpré, and playing piano there to earn his supper.

Later, when Shearing finally relinquished the piano keys, Roy sat down and filled the room with Chopin and

Debussy. Everyone clustered around the piano, murmuring appreciation, and I was ecstatic.

I cornered Price and asked if he remembered a Beverly Hills art gallery that showed Matisse paintings in 1952.

"You and I were the only viewers in the room."

I wasn't going to remind him of our conversation about *House of Wax*.

"Is that a fact," he replied.

"I was wearing a blue-and-white checked dress, and you were completely taken up with the paintings."

"Was I?"

Clearly, he didn't want to talk about that day. No doubt he didn't even remember it.

It was thirty years after the FBI called me to ask about Huey Newton that I read *Shadow Of The Panther*. Written by Hugh Pearson, it came out in 1994. I was anxious to read it because not only was I interested in the group, I was curious about how Huey had changed since junior high.

The book was a revelation, and not in a good way. Besides being co-founder of the Black Panthers (with Bobby Seale), Huey was a cocaine addict, an abuser of women, and a multiple murderer. Now I'd invited him into my home, and how in God's name was I going to handle it?

My heart was pumping like a jackhammer. I put my hand up to my necklace, hoping for an infusion of Dorthy Moxley's courage. As soon as I touched it, I began to calm down.

When Huey first arrived, like the other guests he didn't know why he was here, and even though the thought was politically incorrect, I hoped he would gravitate to Vernon Alley. Vernon always made everyone feel comfortable. Just don't ask him about his freckles.

"We knew each other a long time ago, Huey," I said. "Do you remember me?"

He had grown into a very handsome man, what we used to call a heartthrob.

"Were you at Woodrow Wilson? Are you Miss Hoig, my homeroom teacher?"

"Yes. And I'm glad you came today!"

"Didn't have much choice," Huey mumbled. "They said I had to."

"Who said—"

We were interrupted by Lord Alexander Hesketh, who glided in carrying a huge bouquet of red roses. We embraced, then went to find Ed. After that, I went to the kitchen to find a vase for the flowers.

Since I was busy with the flowers, Mollie went to the door when Doel Reed arrived. She took him around, making introductions. I didn't see him right away, and when I did, I said, "I'm so glad you became so successful, Professor Reed! No one deserves it more!"

"Someone said you married an artist."

"Not only that, I became one!"

Then, recalling his avid interest in my love life, I asked, "Have you met my husband? What do you think?"

He gave me a sideways look. "He seems much older than you."

"Oh, but Professor. Reed, I'm old too. I'm only young for today!"

I pointed to where his aquatint of the chapel in New Mexico was hanging, and he edged closer to study it. I'd forgotten what an imposing figure he was, with his bald head, hooded eyes, and long-limbed frame.

Alex Hesketh called from across the room, and I skittered toward him, moving with a buoyancy of movement I'd never experienced before. I was practically airborne!

"You're a marvelous hostess," he said. "Makes me wish I'd brought my fiancé. And do you have any more of those delicious cream puffs?"

The party was well underway. The music helped loosen everyone up and the room was almost filled with bodies. Cigarette smoke hung in the air, since several of the notables smoked. They knew nothing of the social stigma that smoking carries now, so I didn't say anything, just kept opening windows and doors.

As I moved from group to group passing stuffed mushrooms, I tried to draw out anyone who might not be mixing in. William Scranton and Huey were the quietist; I didn't worry about anyone else. I didn't know Scranton's interests. But since he'd been in politics, I thought of asking him to lead a discussion on Donald Trump. That always makes a party go. I changed my mind, because many of our guests had probably never heard of Trump, and no doubt Scranton hadn't either.

I regretted not inviting my cousin Fran. She wasn't any deader than anyone else, and she would have been so pleased to see Governor Scranton. We could have laughed all over again about our brief foray into politics.

Minutes passed, and I was standing in the dining room all alone. Thinking about the Cow Palace fiasco, and high as a kite from the events of the day, I suddenly went into a fit of uncontrollable giggling. My shoulders shook, and I was almost crying from sheer exhilaration.

Ed rushed into the room. "Calm down! This is going to take years off your life! Sit down somewhere and rest!"

I didn't want to sit down. I was feeling crazily euphoric, and wanted to squeeze every bit of enjoyment I could from the occasion. But even though I'd stopped the hysterical laughter, I was shaking, and I knew Ed was right.

I decided that what I needed was fresh air.

I walked out the back door and started along a garden path until I came to a koi pond. It was a beautiful sight—sparkling water, with six koi and a host of water lilies.

I stood on the edge, trying to breathe more deeply.

Next to the pond was a small cedar gazebo, and inside it sat Mr. Nakamura.

"May I join you?" I asked.

He nodded.

"Do you like our koi pond?"

"All of your garden is wonderful. You are a very fortunate lady."

"I'm afraid it won't be here tomorrow," I said sadly.

Instead of asking me to explain, he said, "I am wondering, why did you create this *kai* today? This gathering?"

I didn't answer right away.

I had thought it was to satisfy my desire to intermingle all these fascinating people, but maybe there was more to it than that.

"I haven't told anyone, Mr. Nakamura, and I hadn't even realized it myself, but I think it's to *remember*. Everything happens so fast, children growing up, careers beginning or ending, friends dying—I wanted to slow it all down and try and figure it out."

"Life is a candle before the wind."

"You mean—?"

"Life is precious and fragile, and can be extinguished at any time."

He turned his head away, and I gazed at his profile.; His eyes were half closed, his expression relaxed but sad.

Mr. Nakamura was such a simple, humble man, and I loved him.

"I know that's true," I said. "I lost a friend unexpectedly the other day. Carole was so young!"

"And so you must enjoy the gathering today. Now let us go inside. As yet, I have not met all of your amazing friends."

I put my arm around his shoulders, and we walked back to the house.

Huey Newton had grown up, and now he was tall and slightly husky.

Mollie and Huey were engrossed in conversation, and I noticed that even though she was grinning, he wasn't. A smile seemed entirely foreign to his expression.

I wondered why Huey was the only guest who'd grown older. But this gathering was a fantasy, all in my imagination, so I must *want* him to be an adult.

But why? Was it guilt because I had never talked to him at Woodrow Wilson, tried to 'bring him out'? Never once interacted with the boy who'd been such a sad, silent figure?

A stark truth hit me.

Maybe Huey, and other poor black boys like him, were the inspiration for the African-American boys I'd written about in my novels. In *The Wind Came Running*, Carlton is athletically gifted but uncommunicative; in *The Putneyville Fables*, Jeff, who is biracial, struggles to find his place in the world.

Whatever the reason, here was Huey, a full-fledged adult. He was standing near the musicians, and I went over to him. "What did you mean by saying 'They said I had to?'"

"I don't know—this voice or somethin'—like I needed to do someone a favor. Was it you? I had to come back?"

My brother Stan arrived last of all. Stan was scrawny as a boy, but now he looked slender and handsome in a dark suit and tie. We kissed and hugged, and he said, "Why'd you invite me to a party without Pat? Why just me?"

"I only invited the famous people I wrote about, and you're one of 'em."

At that, he straightened his shoulders, adjusted his tie, and said, "Well, thanks. I guess I'll try to meet everyone."

My brother had always fancied himself a ladies' man. He hovered on the edge of the crowd of men surrounding Mercedes, then gave up and began talking with Ellie Shearing. They settled down, wineglasses in hand, on our new posh window seat.

Stan seemed dazzled by Ellie. No wonder, she looked gorgeous, wearing a low-cut black blouse and zebra-striped Capri pants.

It was only an hour since the party began, and already things were getting out of control, food and drink-wise.

I felt someone brush against my elbow, and it was Ed Mackay. "Would you like me to help keep the wine going? I'm good at it!"

"Of course, that would be very helpful!"

He sailed off in the direction of the kitchen. The next time I saw him, he was filling George Balanchine's glass, and they were chuckling together like old schoolmates. He kept coming and going from the kitchen with trays of filled glasses, and I was grateful for his help, but when he'd been at it too long, I said, "Better get back to your bass-playing, Ed. I want you to have fun!"

He grinned and relinquished the tray.

I glanced around. Doel Reed and Maury Logan were taking a look at each other's art. Mr. Reed was pointing to his aquatint, probably describing his printing process for Maury. Later on, I saw my old professor roguishly plying Mercedes with a cherry tomato. Some things never change.

After an hour of jazz, I summoned the courage to ask Noel Coward to sing "Mad Dogs and Englishmen."

What a showman! He stood near the piano, and the crowd settled down to listen—some sitting, others standing. He delivered the song as if performing for an audience in the West End, and after a round of applause, did two rousing encores.

Alex Hesketh was the perfect party guest, constantly moving around introducing himself, and charming everyone. At one point he said to me, "You rascal! Shame on you for not mentioning you know Noel Coward!"

It would be hard for anyone to follow Coward's performance, but Jeanette MacDonald could do it if anyone could. Slender as always, Jeanette's red hair and large green eyes were still in Technicolor, and her long gown of white silk and pale green tulle emphasized her beauty. She was the same age as when we'd seen her in Las Vegas, 43, but looked thirty-five. No wonder a French journalist had written in the early 1930s:

> *Jeanette MacDonald is not a heartless beauty holding out a tired promise of vague possibilities. Everything in her delicate being hints of real sensual delight and urges you on to ecstasy. Call it sex-appeal if you must. But she has so much more. Her bewitching qualities transcend vulgarity. They elevate dreams and exalt desire.*

And here she was, practically in the flesh, about to sing in *my* living room!

She sang "Will You Remember," and after that, "Song of Love" and "I'll See You Again," sending all of us into a nostalgic mood. Many of the guests had tears in their eyes, as there were in mine.

Jeanette was easily the most beautiful woman here. Mercedes was dramatic-looking but not beautiful, and Mollie was her usual unadorned self. Maria looked as much like a fashion model as a ballerina; dark, with severe features. Ellie Shearing was attractive but no great beauty, while Helen Douglas was completely grey, looking her age.

After Jeanette's performance, I enthused, "Thank you so much!"

"You're welcome! I'm glad to be singing anywhere!"

Vincent Price swooped down. "Dear Jeanette! How unexpected to see you here, of all places!"

"Yes, it's quite strange, isn't it?"

I left them to reminisce about movies and the actor's life, and next in my reverie, Russell sang, "It's a Lovely Day Today." He was in fine voice, and I realized that I had never heard him sing. I was still hoping that he and I could sneak off somewhere for a private tête-à-tête.

Using new-found courage, I asked Price to tell us a horror tale. He at once sprang into the role of enthusiastic entertainer. As soon as he walked to the front of the room, everyone quieted down. He then began to recite an excerpt from Edgar Allan Poe's "The Black Cat," mesmerizing us with his creepy, nasal voice.

After Price's scary tale, I thought a bit of comedy relief was needed, so I asked Dale Robertson to tell a cowboy joke, and handed him a copy of my brother's *Humor of the American Cowboy*. He said he had the book at home, and quickly found an anecdote in the chapter "Cow Country Critters." He did a great job of reading it, and received a loud round of applause. These people were *pros!*

I glanced over at Stan, who gave me a cheery thumbs-up.

I was, again, higher than a kite. I had only had one glass of wine, but the thrill of this gathering and the display of their individual gifts made me feel drunk as a fiddler.

I next asked Melvyn Douglas to perform the courtroom monologue from *Inherit the Wind*, my favorite part of the play.

He said he'd be happy to. He stood before us, opened his arms, and spoke in his sonorous voice:

Yes, there is something holy to me! The power of the individual human mind.

In a child's power to master the multiplication table there is more sanctity than in all your shouted "Amens!" "Holy, Holies!" and "Hosannahs!" An idea is a greater monument than a cathedral. And the advance of man's knowledge is more of a miracle than any sticks turned to snakes, or the parting of waters.

It went on, and when he finished we applauded for several minutes. I felt the urge to hand him another Oscar.

Like a circus ringmaster, I continued orchestrating events. I walked over to Dakin and Mercedes and asked if they would do something from *Death of a Salesman* or *Streetcar Named Desire*. Or maybe something lighter, like a scene from *Private Lives* or *Present Laughter*?

"Noel would be so pleased," I added.

Dakin said how about Shakespeare, maybe a scene from *Taming of the Shrew*?

Mercedes agreed, and they took their places in front of us and began. Their rapid back-and-forth dialogue was sizzling, and when they finished, the room echoed with clapping.

As the applause died down, I heard bumping sounds. I looked around, and to my astonishment, the room had suddenly expanded even more, and Xavier Cugat's orchestra had appeared!

I sank down on the nearest chair. In my most hallucinatory state, I couldn't believe this was happening!

But here they were in front of my eyes: violinists, trumpet-players, tympanists—a score of tuxedoed musicians! It took them a few minutes to set up, then Cugat raised his baton, and they performed three rumbas, "The Lady in Red", "Green Eyes", and "La Bomba."

Mercedes and Governor Scranton jumped up and rhumbaed around the room as if in a sequence from an old movie musical. I was astonished when Alex took the tray out of my helper Sarah's hands, grabbed her in his arms, and began dancing. Sarah was laughing, and they seemed to be having the time of their lives.

After half-an-hour of Latin music, Cugat's band went up in smoke—*POOF!*

I was glad, because there wasn't enough food, although I probably could have conjured up more.

My pal Xavier stayed on.

After the music stopped, everything quieted down, and the guests began to break up into small groups. Some of these groups surprised and thrilled me, giving me a feeling of pleasure that I can't explain. Cugat was in deep conversation with, of all people, J. C. Penney, and Dakin and Maria were having an intimate moment. He was stroking her arm as if hoping some of her magic would rub off.

When I glimpsed Henry Koerner walk Mollie to a window and turn her face to one side as if deciding the best angle for a portrait, I was surprised, but I knew he was forever thinking like an artist.

Perched together on a loveseat, Steven Zellerbach and Mercedes were in deep conversation, and Charles Schulz sat alone by a window, stroking Shammy's ears.

Mollie had told me that she'd always wanted to meet the creator of "Peanuts," so I took her away from Koerner and over to Schulz. They immediately connected, and I heard her ask if he ever got tired of deadlines. He thought for a moment and said, "No, never. I loved my characters, and was probably happiest when I was drawing them."

At long last, I had a private moment with Russell. Somehow we landed in the kitchen, and my helpers were nowhere around.

If there is anything more sweetly nostalgic than a revisited love affair, it's a visit to a never-begun one. When I asked, he said he remembered the time in Belvedere when we swam in the pool, sipped Bloody Marys, and chatted about a dead sex goddess.

I kept reminding myself that, to Russell, I still looked young, maybe even desirable. I was thankful he couldn't see me as I really am.

He took my hand, and when I laughed I sounded like a young girl.

"I asked if you ever got involved with your leading ladies," I said. *"I blush to think of it!"*

"I was wondering, my dear, why you included me today. I'm certainly not well-known anymore."

"You're still a star to me!"

Just then a shooting pain attacked my left hip.

"How about a stick of celery stuffed with pimiento cheese?"

"No thanks." He put his hand on my shoulder. "Have you been happy?"

"Uh-huh. Yes. Had a couple of kids."

"I remember."

Neither of us spoke for several seconds.

I could have stood there with him 'til the cows came home. Instead I said, "I should get back to the others."

"I can't get over meeting Noel Coward!"

"Me neither."

He pressed my hand to his heart, and like Hamlet's ghost, I evanesced into the living room, and there were Vernon and Maria together on a sofa. Her hair, adorned with white feathers, was swept up and away from her marvelous cheekbones, while Charles Schulz, in rapt attention, leaned close. That was the only time I saw Maria smile. I even heard her laugh, with the rippling, throaty sound of a diva.

I offered paté to Dale Robertson and Helen Douglas, plumped a cushion behind J. C. Penney's back; and fetched an aspirin for Vincent Price, who told me Cugat's percussion section had given him a headache.

George Shearing and Cynthia were in the midst of a conversation with their fellow Brit, Noel Coward. George and Noel, longtime showbiz veterans, had of course crossed paths many times.

A half-hour later, the women were all bunched together, and I decided to join them. Ellie was saying she was worried about George's recent hospitalization, and Helen was talking about the many separations she and Melvyn had endured because of their careers, he in Hollywood and she in Washington. While she chatted, I mused about her reported affair with LBJ, and wondered how it had impacted her marriage. Melvyn, too, might have succumbed to temptation during their times apart. I'd always wondered about him and Garbo, since they made several movies together.

Helen and Jeanette began discussing opera. Jeanette spoke about performing opera in Canada and America, but sounding regretful, said that she could never make it to the Metropolitan in New York.

When Helen Douglas said she'd studied voice for two years and afterward toured Europe singing various operatic roles, I noticed a look of envy cloud Jeanette's face.

How could that be? She was immensely rich and, in her day, the most famous soprano in the world.

Does jealousy last past the grave?

It was too big a subject for me to ponder, so I got up and began circling the room again.

Paul Mills and Vincent Price were standing in front of Doel Reed's "Ranchos Church." Price was gesturing enthusiastically, his headache seemingly forgotten, and Paul was nodding in agreement.

Like birds on a wire, the three old guys, Reed, Penney, and Logan sat silently next to each other on a long sofa. Why weren't they conversing? I suddenly realized they were probably all deaf, so conversation may have been difficult.

The jazz trio was playing "Lullaby in Birdland," and in the center of the room, another elderly gent was holding a group enthralled. Noel Coward was relating a raucous tale about Gertrude Lawrence. I wanted to stop and listen, but the next thing I knew the scene had changed, and I was outdoors!

Russell, Ed Mackay, and I were strolling along with our wineglasses, and I seemed to be floating spellbound in the presence of the two charmers. We found an outdoor table under a weeping willow tree which didn't used to be there, sat down, and began talking about the past. Ed said with a sigh, "The Reagan days, those were the golden years!"

"Do you really think so?" said Russell. "To me, the '60s and '70s were the great years! Of course, that was when I was busiest with my career."

"A lot of that time is a blur," I said. "It was when we were raising our kids, and I was caught up in that."

Both men gave me a look.

"Aren't you a bit forgetful, my child?" said Ed. "Seems to me you were a bit of a party girl!"

"Oh no, that wasn't the real me!"

Russell said, "Let's toast to past days, shall we?"

We clinked glasses, making a reverberating *'ting!'* which echoed on and on.

Russell smiled, Ed chuckled, and I glowed with other-worldly bliss.

So far the party had been a delightful flight of fancy, but there were several rude jolts to come.

Just as I was thanking Providence that everything had worked out so smoothly, while carrying my biggest serving tray, I collided—*BAM!*—with Vincent Price. The tray held a load of food and drink; at the moment of impact, along with twenty filled coffee mugs, it held a plate of prawns and a dish filled with onion dip.

Why couldn't I have run into my husband, or Mollie! I'm not sure about Ed, but Mollie would have forgiven me right away. But no, my victim had to be Price.

"Good God!" he sputtered, looking down at his perfectly creased trousers, now sodden with liquid and plastered with dip.

"Oh! I'm so sorry!" I wailed. At our feet lay pieces of broken crockery, with a half-gallon of coffee seeping into the rug.

I yelled, *"Ladies!"* and magically, my helpers came and started cleaning it up.

Ed was three inches shorter than the actor, but I said, "I'll find another pair of trousers, wait here."

Price began to blot his pants with a damp dish towel, and I left for the bedroom. I found some chinos that might fit him, and was on my way back when I came upon two people embracing in the hallway. The expression on Steven

Zellerbach's face as he stroked Jeanette's cheek was so nakedly lovesick, I had to look away. She glanced up, and our eyes met. I wanted to say, "You've still got it, sweetie!" but I only smiled and slipped past.

I suppose if old folks can fall for each other in a nursing home which, reportedly, they do all the time, they can fall in love after they're—well, *you* know.

Price elected to keep wearing his own trousers, and seeing that he'd calmed down, I left him to check on my old guys again. Only two were still on the sofa. Maury was dozing with Shammy on his lap, and Doel Reed was half-awake, staring into space.

Where was Mr. Penney? I found Mollie and asked if she'd seen him, and she said she thought she saw him go out the back door.

"All by himself?"

"Yes, why?"

"It's okay, I'll find him."

On the far side of the garden near our beautiful new purple rhododendron, Mercedes was walking along with Balanchine and Cugat. Both men were shorter than the actress by several inches, but no one seemed to care. Cugat was placing a flower behind her ear while Balanchine grasped her arm, pointing up to something he wanted her to see.

A bird? A plane? Superman?

There was no sign of Mr. Penney, so I went back inside, then out on the deck, where I found Noel Coward in our canvas butterfly chair. His black tie was askew, his formal dinner clothes wrinkled. Half an hour before, at his request, I had prepared a third martini, and now he was sound asleep, looking as innocent as a sleeping babe.

I asked Mollie to get him hot coffee, then found Ed. "I can't locate Mr. Penney. Did you see him leave?"

"No, but I'll take care of it. Sit down and stop running around! You look awful, and you're going to pay for this—you'll have to spend a week in bed!"

Roy Bogas said he'd seen Penney disappear through the trees bordering our property, so he and Ed went to find him. Ten minutes later, they walked Penney back to the house and deposited him on the sofa.

"Where was he?" I whispered.

"Sitting on a tree stump out past the gardening shed. I think he got lost," said Ed.

"In *our* garden?"

"It seems to be very large today! Maybe he wanted to have some peace and quiet away from all the noise."

"Yes, you musicians make a terrible racket!"

Ed looked exhausted too. He would never admit it, though, wouldn't stop playing trombone 'til he dropped.

Not long after that, Cynthia and Bishop Pike were taking an arm-in-arm stroll down a garden path, and suddenly the Bishop ran into our new stone bird bath. Engrossed in conversation with Cynthia, he got knocked down by the bird bath, then couldn't get up. Cynthia wasn't able to pull him upright, so she rushed into the house and enlisted my husband's help. Ed brought him inside, and we found that the Bishop wasn't injured, just disheveled and very, very embarrassed.

Another rude reality was headed my way. I had wanted to talk to Huey and try to thrash out a few things, but since I was one of those teachers who 'tried to rob him of the sense of his own uniqueness and worth,' I decided he probably wouldn't want to have a serious conversation with me.

Maybe he'd like to discuss race relations with someone else. The only guests who might want to take part in a conversation like that were the Douglases, famous for their liberal views, so I found them and asked them to do me a favor and chat with Huey.

Huey was with Vernon outside at a picnic table. Shammy was there, in her element, begging for food. I sat down with an open bottle of Louis Latour chardonnay, and soon Melvyn and Helen joined us.

Huey was talking about police brutality in America, listing aloud some of the black men killed in encounters with authority in the last few years.

"Michael Brown, Tamir Rice, Walter Scott, Bobby Hutton, Luther Jackson. Roman Ducksworth Jr.—and those're just a very few of the brothers who've been killed at the hands of the police. Now there are cameras everywhere recording police crimes, and thank God for that! We didn't create the Black Panthers to ramp up hate for white people, like everyone says. We did it to keep brothers from gettin' murdered!"

Helen Douglas spoke up. "When I was in Washington, I worked on the Civil Rights Commission, and we ran a survey that said—"

Huey interrupted. "I don't suppose you know much about it!"

Ignoring him, she went on to make some crucial points, how in the '50s, employment for African Americans began improving, and how blacks are now accepted in all the services and all sports.

"That's bullshit," Huey growled. "Where you been? That stuff all happened way, way back. Brothers are still kept out of neighborhoods and golf clubs all over the country! And don't give me no fuckin' Tiger Woods stories!"

He was lighting one cigarette after another, taking only a few puffs on each. "We're still gettin' shot for the smallest infringements of the law!"

He removed a silver flask from his pocket and took a long swallow, then stood up and started circling the table. He seemed agitated, reminding me of a description I'd read in Pearson's book.

> *Friends constantly remarked on how wound up he seemed. He couldn't sit still, and the imagery of the Panther suited him because he always seemed ready to pounce.*

Vernon said soothingly, "Things are better now, kid, you gotta admit it."

"Why have I gotta admit it? I'm *right*, ol' man, and you know it!"

He plopped down, looking sullen and unhappy.

Melvyn Douglas entered the fray.

In a confident voice, he said, "Statistics show that in the last ten years, there have been vast improvements in employment rates for blacks. It's education that seems to be the sticking point." He cleared his throat. "Colleges and graduate schools are filled with minorities, but poor blacks—those from the ghettos of Oakland and Detroit and Chicago, simply aren't being educated."

I was glad to hear Douglas vent his views and was sorry I had to leave the discussion, but it was time for dessert.

My helpers and I got ready to pass my home-made brownies. I carried a trayful into the living room, where Shearing was playing and singing, "It Never Entered My Mind."

I had to sit down and listen. I looked over at Ed, who was enjoying the moment as much as I was, and we exhanged a grin.

Earlier, for the *piece de resistance*, I had asked Maria to dance, and she promised she would. The shock of her acquiescence almost caused me to wake up, but then I remembered—*this is a fantasy!*—and managed to remain in my other-worldly state.

I went to Roy Bogas and asked if he would accompany her, saying she would probably want Stravinsky or Prokofiev.

"I would be honored," he said.

I went back to the kitchen for more brownies, and when I glanced outside, saw Vernon and Huey still sitting at the outdoor table. Huey's head had dropped into his arms, and he looked as if he might pass out.

Vernon stood up and came toward the house. Entering the kitchen, he said, "How about some coffee? My pal needs it."

"Sure," I said. "Poor Huey! I thought things would be different for him today, but I guess not."

Giving me a look that combined both sympathy and exasperation, he said, "I want to thank you for inviting me today, honey, but last time I checked, this ain't heaven."

He patted my back. "I'd appreciate it if you'd give me a cup, too. Cream and sugar."

I poured two coffees and said, "I hope you'll both come inside. Maria Tallchief is going to dance, and you shouldn't miss it!"

"We'll be in pretty soon." Carrying the two coffees, he walked back outdoors. I was relieved to see Mollie sit down at the table, take the mug from Vernon, and slowly bring it to Huey's lips.

Back in the living room, Ellie approached me.

"I have a favor to ask. Today is George's birthday—it's 2019, and he's ninety-nine! I'd like to sing 'Happy

Birthday,' so I was wondering, could Roy play it for me? I think George has forgotten it's his big day!"

"Sure, I'll try to herd everyone in. Do you want to do it right now?"

"Yes, please."

"Okay, give me a second."

I went back to the kitchen, looked in the freezer and found a frozen cupcake. I stuck a red candle in it, lit it, and went back.

Roy struck a chord, and Ellie began to sing, *"Happy Birthday to you! Happy Birthday to you! Happy Birthday, dear Ge-o-r-o-orge, Happy Birthday to you!"*

Everyone joined in—all these famous people who had never met until today—and we sang together. After that, Ellie took the lit cupcake to George and said, "Make a wish!"

He blew it out, and suddenly the room went completely dark.

With the sounds of "Happy Birthday" echoing in my ears, I woke up. The cooing of doves from the garden softened my reentry to the real world.

Damn! I knew getting to see Tallchief dance was too good to be true!

There were sounds from the kitchen, so Ed was up.

I felt something small and hard pressing against my hip, so I reached under the covers and brought out a partially-burnt red candle.

George's birthday candle!

Ed walked in carrying two mugs of coffee.

Wasn't someone else just doing that?

"Good morning," he said, looking handsome in his blue-striped pajamas. He kissed me on the cheek. "How'd you get cookie crumbs on your pillow? You never eat in bed!"

I turned my head. There they were, a cluster of chocolate crumbs.

'Oh, the brownies!"

"What brownies?"

I brushed the crumbs into a wastebasket. "Wait a second. Would you mind not talking just yet? I had the most marvelous dream, and I'm trying to remember it."

Bless his soul! Understanding the strange quirks and whims of a writer, he left the room.

I arranged several pillows behind my back and sat propped up in bed, concentrating.

Dreams are so ephemeral! They can be gone in a mini-second, and my fantasy dream was fast disappearing.

I found paper and pen in a nightstand, took a deep breath, and began to write it all down.

About the Author

Marianne Gage is a San Francisco Bay Area artist, teacher, and writer.

Her first novel, *The Wind Came Running,* was a coming-of-age story set in her native Oklahoma. After that came *The Putneyville Fables,* with a plot revolving around a Colorado family's involvement with animals.

Her latest novel, *All Kinds of Beauty*, explores the joys and heartbreaks of life-long friendships and the process of an artist in search of herself.

Marianne has given readings at Bay Area book clubs, and has made appearances at Book Passage Bookstore in Corte Madera, California as well as the Ferry Building in San Francisco.

She was married for 68 years to the distinguished San Francisco artist and illustrator Ed Diffenderfer.

Acknowledgments

I would like to thank my wonderful editor
and literary midwife—patient, productive, and extremely
accomplished Karen Mireau Rimmer.

Without her, this book would never
have come to fruition.

To learn more
about the Author
please visit
MarianneGageBooks.blogspot.com

To contact the Publisher
please email Karen Mireau
Azalea.Art.Press@gmail.com
https://karenmireaubooks.com

www.ingramcontent.com/pod-product-compliance
Lightning Source LLC
Chambersburg PA
CBHW020752160426
43192CB00006B/316